ALEXANDER
& THREE SMALL PLAYS

ALEXANDER
& THREE SMALL PLAYS

BY
LORD DUNSANY

WILDSIDE PRESS

CONTENTS

	PAGE
ALEXANDER	1
THE OLD KING'S TALE	137
THE EVIL KETTLE	157
THE AMUSEMENTS OF KHAN KHARUDA	181

ALEXANDER

DRAMATIS PERSONÆ

ALEXANDER THE GREAT
CLITUS, *his friend*
APOLLO, *in disguise*
NEARCHOS, *an Admiral*
PTOLEMY ⎫
        ⎬ *The Great Captains of Alexander*
PERDICCAS ⎭
A PRIEST OF APOLLO
AN ARCHER
2ND ARCHER
PSEUSTES, *flatterer to* PTOLEMY
SYCOPHANTES, *flatterer to* PERDICCAS
THE AMBASSADOR OF THE HILL-MEN
THE AMBASSADOR OF THE NOMADS
THE AMBASSADOR OF THE ARABS
A RHETORICIAN
THAIS
THE QUEEN OF THE AMAZONS
THE THREE FATES

Retinues, Heralds, Soldiers, Amazons, etc., etc.

ALEXANDER

ACT I

Scene: Persepolis, and the fallen statue of Xerxes.
[Enter ALEXANDER, NEARCHOS, *and* APOLLO *disguised as man.]*

ALEXANDER
At last, Persepolis.

NEARCHOS
O Alexander, it is Persepolis.

ALEXANDER
And you, O fallen image with the tiara of Persia on your head, who are you?

NEARCHOS
Indeed, I think it is the statue of Xerxes.

ALEXANDER
Xerxes. Indeed, it is a piteous thing to see lie thus one who has held a sceptre.

NEARCHOS
It is only an old statue.

ALEXANDER

But think. It is the statue of great Xerxes, whose feet so many kissed. Now it lies here and no one sets it up.

NEARCHOS

That is a shameful thing. We are his enemies. But that the Persians do not guard their king, though he is dead and in the shadow of war, is a shameful thing.

ALEXANDER

I would set him up.

NEARCHOS

Yet he brought war into our sacred land and filled with weeping all the valleys of Greece.

ALEXANDER

I cannot tell whether I should pass by you and let you lie, for the war you made sometime against the Grecians, or whether I should lift you up, respecting the noble mind and virtues you had.

APOLLO

Do not set it up.

[ALEXANDER *nods and turns from it.*]

VOICES OFF

A judgment. A judgment.

[*Enter* ARXES. *He kneels.*]

ACT I *ALEXANDER*

ALEXANDER
Ah. What is your name?

ARXES
Arxes, your Grace. For ten years in the company of Kylos, a Macedonian soldier, and now a commander of ten.

ALEXANDER
And friend of Alexander, as all good soldiers are. What would you have of me?

ARXES
A judgment, your Grace. We have a prisoner here taken yesterday in the battle in the monstrous act of aiming at Alexander—an archer who had come most nigh your Grace, most nigh, and aiming surely.

[PRISONER *is dragged on.*]

ALEXANDER
I thank you for your zeal, my zealous Arxes. Are there any among the prisoners the gods gave us who did not aim at Alexander?

[*A manacled* PRISONER *rushes forward.*]

MANACLED PRISONER
Your most High Grace, I did not aim at you, I did not aim at you. I did not aim at your godlike Majesty.

ALEXANDER ACT I

ALEXANDER
Why not?

MANACLED PRISONER
Your most high Grace, I durst not.

ALEXANDER
Your served Darius ill. Let him be flogged, my Arxes; but clemently and with the single whip. [*He turns to the other* ARCHER.] But to you, since it pleased the gods to give me Persia, I stand on behalf of Darius, and in Darius's name I give you the golden chain, that a good soldier may not miss his reward.
[ALEXANDER *walks away.* PRISONER *remains kneeling.*]

ARXES
[*To* PRISONER, *scratching his head*]: Well, Prisoner, it seems I'm an old fool.
[*Exeunt.*]
2ND SOLDIER [*pointing with open hand and extended arm.*]
What must we do with these, O Alexander?

ALEXANDER
To these we are what the high gods are to us.

2ND SOLDIER
We smite them then.

ACT I *ALEXANDER*

ALEXANDER

No. When the gods have smitten the world with thunder and the crops can endure no more, how often do they astonish us with rainbows. The gods are clement.

2ND SOLDIER

We must not punish them?

ALEXANDER

Let Darius punish those that ran away. But these that fought us to the last let them go home and see their wives again.

CAPTIVES

Oh-h Alexander!

ALEXANDER

Tell the Persians.

THAIS [*drunk*]

Burn Persepolis, Alexander. Burn Persepolis. Bid us burn Persepolis.

ALEXANDER

You are drunken, Thais, and it is not yet evening.

THAIS

Do not taunt me with being drunken when you are the cause, Alexander.

ALEXANDER

ALEXANDER
How am I the cause of your drunkenness, good Thais?

THAIS
It was to celebrate your victory.

ALEXANDER
Farewell, my merry Thais. I go to consult with my captains.

CLITUS
My lovely Thais. [*Approaches her.*]

THAIS [*to* APOLLO]
Old man, dance with me.
[APOLLO *walks straight on, but looks at her terribly.*]
[*Recoiling.*] Don't look at me with your eyes like that!
[*Exeunt* ALEXANDER, NEARCHOS, APOLLO.]

THAIS
Do you love me, Clitus?

CLITUS
Yes, Thais, surely I love you.

THAIS
Do you always love me, Clitus?

ACT I *ALEXANDER*

CLITUS
Yes, I always love you.

THAIS
Ptolemy did not use to love me always. He only loved me when I was sober.

CLITUS
I love you always.

THAIS
If you love me, Clitus, why then you will do a little thing for me.

CLITUS
A little thing, Thais?

THAIS
Indeed, but a little thing.

CLITUS
I will do what you will.

THAIS [*clutching him*]
That old man, Clitus! That terrible old man! Send him away, Clitus. I—I—I do not like the old man.

CLITUS
Nay, but he hath the ear of Alexander. He is indeed as his shadow. In all his battles he has

ALEXANDER ACT I

been at his elbow, in the council hall he is there. I cannot send him away.

THAIS

You know that Alexander would give his life for you, Clitus, or even all his kingdoms. Has he refused you aught since you were boys and ran together on the hills of Greece?

CLITUS

No. He is generous. But this is not reasonable. Why do you not like the old man, Thais? He ever advises Alexander wisely.

THAIS

I do not like him.

CLITUS

But he does not harm you.

THAIS

He looks at me.

CLITUS

We all look at you, Thais.

THAIS

He looks at me. And when he looks at me he sees all the things that I have ever done and all the things I will do.

ACT I *ALEXANDER*

CLITUS
I am sure they were all most good, the things you have done.

THAIS
They were evil things.

CLITUS
No, no, Thais.

THAIS
He looks at me and he sees them.

CLITUS
But you bade him dance with you.

THAIS
I was drunken.

CLITUS
Nay, you are sober, Thais.

THAIS
He looked at me, and I am terribly sober, and full of a great thirst.

CLITUS
I fear lest an evil fall upon our army if I should do this thing.

THAIS
What evil should happen?

ALEXANDER — ACT I

CLITUS

He might go away and never return again.

THAIS

Why should he not?

CLITUS

He has been so long a time with Alexander. He has been in our councils since we first left Greece, and no one knows his name.

THAIS

Doth not Alexander know it?

CLITUS

He hath never spoken it, Thais, even to me.

THAIS

There is something strange about that, mark you, there is something strange about that.

CLITUS

It is a business I would have no hand in.

THAIS

If you do not send him away you do not love me, and I will surely die and forget the evil things that I have done.

CLITUS

No, no, Thais, I love you and you must never die. What would become of us if you left us, Thais. But I cannot——

ACT I *ALEXANDER*

THAIS

I will not have him look at me with his eyes. I would sooner die and forget the things I have done. Why does he look at me?

CLITUS

But, Thais.

THAIS

I tell you I will die. I will die, Clitus. He shall not look at me.

CLITUS

But, Thais, be calm; do not cry out but hear me——

THAIS

I will die, die, die. Farewell, Clitus, I will drown myself——

CLITUS

No, but you must not.

THAIS

I will drown myself down in a huge quiet lake, full of soft weeds, and he shall not look at me.

CLITUS

No, Thais!

THAIS

Farewell!

CLITUS
Thais, I will send him away.

THAIS
You will send him away, Clitus?

CLITUS
I will send the old man away. I will ask Alexander.

THAIS
You promise me.

CLITUS
I promise. I will ask Alexander.

[THAIS *draws his sword.*]

THAIS
Promise me by your sword that the old man shall go.

CLITUS
He shall go, Thais.

[*He touches the blade that* THAIS *holds towards him.*]

THAIS
My Clitus.

CLITUS
But we must hear no more of lovely Thais dying. That would be terrible. What should we do?

ACT I *ALEXANDER*

THAIS

No, Clitus.

CLITUS

I would fain not ask so much of Alexander. Yet I have promised.

THAIS

You have promised.

[*Enter* ALEXANDER.]

ALEXANDER

Clitus. My dear friend, Clitus.

CLITUS

Alexander.

ALEXANDER

The gods have given us a noble victory.

CLITUS

Indeed, you took it for yourself with your own good sword, Alexander.

ALEXANDER

No, Clitus: give praise unto the gods alone. What is man with his boasts who lies so soon like that? [*Pointing at* Xerxes.]

CLITUS

But all men praise you as equal unto the gods.

ALEXANDER ACT I

ALEXANDER
Praise the gods only.

CLITUS
O Alexander, would you still grant me anything I desired?

ALEXANDER
O Clitus, for what cause do you ask me this? Have I grown miserly? Have I forgot our friendship? That is an unkind question, Clitus.

CLITUS
Indeed I know you. Were you not generous you were not Alexander. But it is a hard boon that I desire and one difficult to grant. Therefore I asked the question.

ALEXANDER
Why ask a little thing of Alexander? And is it hard for me to grant a boon to my dear friend?

CLITUS
O Alexander, I ask not for myself, but there are those that murmur against that old man who is ever in your councils. I pray you dismiss him and lead us henceforth alone.

ALEXANDER
I would that you had asked me some other boon.

ACT I   *ALEXANDER*

Thais

You have sworn, Clitus.

Clitus

I would that I might ask no boon of you, Alexander. And yet I ask for this. And surely alone and without councillors you could govern the world.

Alexander

What man can stand alone?

Clitus

Surely you, Alexander.

Alexander

Praise no man. Listen, Clitus [ALEXANDER *sits down on some fallen pillar or stone*], and I will tell you what I have told to none; a thing that none have guessed. It was on the hills in Hellas when I was young. I was not quite sixteen. You know the road that comes from Lacedæmon, the way the heralds take that go to Delphi?

Clitus

Yes, I remember.

Alexander

I was hunting once along the hills beside it with my two hounds Hermes and Hades—do you remember them?

CLITUS

I well remember them.

ALEXANDER

We had not found a wolf all day and it was nearing evening, when I saw an old man coming down the road looking to the left and to the right as he went, as one who searched for something. He came quite near me. I said: "For what are you searching, O old man?" He said: "I search for one who shall be beautiful and brave and strong." He said I was beautiful. I said I was brave. So he said: "Look me in the eyes." And I looked long in them though he had terrible eyes. He said I had great bravery, but what of my strength. I said: "Test it, O old man," and he held out his little finger and bade me bend it. It was an hour to sunset. I wrestled with the old man's little finger, and just at sunset I bent it a little downwards. He said I had terrible strength. And then he promised me, on the road that runs to Delphi, that because I was beautiful and brave and strong he would go with me always as long as I should wish, and tell me at all times, however slight the occasion, which of two courses it were best to follow.

CLITUS

And this is that strange old man?

ALEXANDER

Even he. And he hath counselled me with wisdom at all times.

ACT I   *ALEXANDER*

CLITUS

Yet sometimes his schemes err, surely.

ALEXANDER

No, Clitus.

CLITUS

But all men err a little, however great their wisdom.

ALEXANDER

O Clitus, this old man is the god Apollo.

CLITUS

The god Apollo!

THAIS

You swore by your sword, Clitus.

CLITUS

The god Apollo.

ALEXANDER

Even he, Clitus.

THAIS

By your sword.

CLITUS

It will be said years hence of Alexander: "He was but a piece upon the board of one of the

ALEXANDER

games of Apollo which he plays with Destiny or some other god, as it were a game of chess which the Egyptians play."

ALEXANDER

We are all, Clitus, pieces in that game.

CLITUS

Not Alexander.

ALEXANDER

Yes, Clitus, I no less than all men else.

CLITUS

Yet you love glory, Alexander.

ALEXANDER

Yes, I love glory. It is the light of a man. It is to a man what its radiance is to a lantern. It proceeds out of him. Without it he were worthless.

CLITUS

O Alexander, you have conquered kings. This other men have done. But none has stepped before from the destined scheme to play themselves as the Egyptians play. This were to conquer gods.

ALEXANDER

This is not talk for men. It is enough for us to conquer kings.

ACT I *ALEXANDER*

CLITUS

No, Alexander. Apollo conquers kings. It is an idle game that he plays with Destiny.

ALEXANDER

True, Clitus. I had forgotten. We do nothing.

CLITUS

In the old stories that the ancients tell did a man ever gain by the gifts of the gods? Have they not ever sought some crafty end, giving to man in usury?

ALEXANDER

Apollo gave me victories and good counsel.

CLITUS

The gods feared Alexander. And so he came fawning and full of guile to ingratiate himself and make you his servant?

ALEXANDER

And why not, Clitus? We must serve the gods.

CLITUS

The gods fear you.

ALEXANDER

Apollo gives me victories.

CLITUS

He gives you little victories. World-girdling Apollo fears for his dominion. If you went on without him you would conquer the world. Why! Men would worship you in torrid India and even forget Apollo.

ALEXANDER

Can we do so much, Clitus?

CLITUS

Let us test it.

ALEXANDER

That were daring.

CLITUS

The world shall wonder at you when it forgets the gods.

ALEXANDER

Yet would I not do it but for you, Clitus.

CLITUS

And indeed I would not ask it but for——

[ALEXANDER *goes out signing to* APOLLO, *who follows.*]

[*With violent remorse.*] The thing is done. Thais! The thing is done! I have thwarted Destiny. I have hindered the gods!

ACT I *ALEXANDER*

THAIS

Calm yourself, Clitus. I bade you do it.

CLITUS

You! What is the airy Thais that the gods should blame her or the world remember? No, it is I. I have altered the fate of the world.

THAIS

No, Clitus. Rest your mind. The gods gave the fate of the world to a woman, Clitus.

CLITUS

To a woman? What woman, Thais?

THAIS

Any woman. The gods care not. It is the way of the gods.

CLITUS

My little Thais, you speak of things you cannot understand.

[*Enter* DANCERS.]

A LEADER OF THE DANCE

The dull old man is dismissed. We shall have revels now.

THAIS [*starting up*]

He is dismissed? You say he is dismissed?

Leader of the Dance
Alexander has sent him away.

Thais
And the old man, has he left him?

Leader of the Dance
Yes. He has put his cloak over his face and is going away angry.

Thais [*kissing him*]
Dear dancer, how sweet your tidings!

Leader of the Dance
Dance with me, Thais.
   [*They dance and all the others drift by behind them.*]
And what shall we do for our little Thais now?

Thais
I think I would have them burn Persepolis.

Leader of the Dance
Persepolis! But, Thais, think what a city!

Thais
Say rather of Greece "what a country"! And was it not from these walls that Xerxes came to make a war upon the holy land?

ACT I *ALEXANDER*

LEADER OF THE DANCE
Yes, long ago.

THAIS
He vexed the fields of Hellas. [*She spits at the fallen image.*] Bah, Xerxes, lie there. Paráxonēs, I have seen many days . . .

LEADER OF THE DANCE
Nay, Thais, that rosy blush is less than twenty summers.

THAIS
It is younger than that, Paráxonēs. I painted it this morning.

LEADER OF THE DANCE
Nay now, Thais, surely—

THAIS
I have seen many days and most were evil, yet once I was a child in the holy land and I remember all the songs of Hellas. Yes, I remember our country. They say I was beautiful then, Paráxonēs.

LEADER OF THE DANCE
Indeed, you are very beautiful, our Thais.

THAIS
Nay, but I was in Hellas, our holy land. None said so but they looked and were very mute and

went their way in silence. I remember that child, that Thais [*getting louder*], and that country; and they that vex it, I will burn their bones, and spit on their images that are fallen low, and burn their city and high memorials down—[*quieter*] for the sake of Hellas.

LEADER OF THE DANCE

Why, Thais, you are angry.

THAIS

No, I am thirsty. Give me some wine, Paráxonēs.

LEADER OF THE DANCE

Wine. Wine for our Thais.

VOICES

Wine. Wine for Thais.

[THAIS *drinks herself stupid. Trumpets sound.*]

DANCERS

Hark, the great captains come.

ANOTHER

That's the great captains.

[*Enter* PTOLEMY *and* PERDICCAS, *great captains of* ALEXANDER.]

PERDICCAS

Thank you, my good Sycophantes. I am afraid you are a sad flatterer. Yet it was well said.

ACT I   *ALEXANDER*

Sycophantes

I flatter no man. But to the demigods I give that reverence that is their due.

Perdiccas

My friend! My friend! No, no. You say too much. I am only poor Perdiccas. [*He sighs.*]
[Pseustes *kneels and offers a cup to* Ptolemy.]

Ptolemy

My good Pseustes, you must not kneel to me.

Pseustes

I kneel, O Ptolemy, because the soothsayer said . . .

Ptolemy

Hush, Pseustes, you must not speak treason.

Pseustes

He said you should be king of Greece and Rome.

Ptolemy

Hush, hush, Pseustes, this is treason.

Pseustes

And that the moon shall be named moon no longer but be known for ever as Ptolemy in your honour.

PTOLEMY
He said too much.

PSEUSTES
And that you shall one day have the command of an army with no superior above you.

PTOLEMY [*sighs*]
These soothsayers sometimes fail to foretell truly.

PSEUSTES
Alas that one so wise and truthful as Ptolemy should so err and say what is false.

PTOLEMY
What!

PSEUSTES
I weep for the ignorance of Ptolemy in this matter.

PTOLEMY
My ignorance?

PSEUSTES
I am no flatterer but say the plain blunt truth. In this matter Ptolemy, so wise, is ignorant.

THAIS
Ptolemy is a fool; and Perdiccas is a fool.

ACT I   *ALEXANDER*

PERDICCAS

What!

PTOLEMY

And what is Thais?

THAIS

Thais, poor fool, knows her folly, being wiser than Ptolemy.

PERDICCAS

Heed her not, Ptolemy, she's drunk.

THAIS

. . . and being wiser than Perdiccas.

CLITUS

Thais! Your folly will undo Alexander! Repent of it and . . .

THAIS

That's the folly of the gods. I told you it was the gods. They are always throwing the world away to some woman. I cannot stop the gods.

PERDICCAS

Let her be. She's drunk.

CLITUS

Ah, I loved Thais and I have ruined the world.

[APOLLO *crosses stage. They taunt him. Exit the rabble after* APOLLO. *The* FLATTERERS *remain.*]

PSEUSTES
So he is gone.

SYCOPHANTES
I will follow after Perdiccas. He lately promised me a cup of gold.

PSEUSTES
Of gold did you say?

SYCOPHANTES
I think it was to be of gold, perhaps it was silver.

PSEUSTES
Perdiccas gives no gold.

SYCOPHANTES
No, it was to be silver, I remember now.

PSEUSTES
I will stay here.

SYCOPHANTES
And does not Ptolemy give you pieces of silver?

PSEUSTES
Alexander gives naught but gold when he makes gifts.

ACT I *ALEXANDER*

SYCOPHANTES

Alexander!

PSEUSTES

And why not, now?

SYCOPHANTES

Will Alexander hear us?

PSEUSTES

Not much at first. But we shall say little at first.

SYCOPHANTES

And then?

PSEUSTES

Is not the old man gone?

SYCOPHANTES

I will *not* follow after Perdiccas.

PSEUSTES

Let Ptolemy find dogs for his silver pieces.

SYCOPHANTES

And what will you say when you praise Alexander?

PSEUSTES

You shall praise him. I will not speak till you have your cup of gold.

ALEXANDER   ACT I

SYCOPHANTES

O generous Pseustes.

PSEUSTES

This is a man worth praising.

SYCOPHANTES

Yet none before have praised him unrebuked.

PSEUSTES

Never before was he free of that old man's counsel. We will find him like a child that is run from school.

SYCOPHANTES

Shall we run and throw one more stone at the queer old man?

PSEUSTES

No, it is going to thunder. [*Flash—another.*] Look! How the lightning flashes along the hills. [*A Flash.*]

SYCOPHANTES

I pray Zeus that it may not strike the army.

PSEUSTES

No. It is going from us from hill to hill. See how it strikes Akneion. That was Shaknos. There's the heath blazing upon Mount Ilaunos, and there on Ebnoth. What a fearful storm!

ACT I   *ALEXANDER*

SYCOPHANTES

I am glad it is going from us. That peal was like
—footsteps.

PSEUSTES

It *was* like footsteps.

SYCOPHANTES [*frightened*]

How terrible are the gods.

PSEUSTES

Zeus, what a storm! And how sudden.

SYCOPHANTES

I thought I saw a shape upon the mountains, a large shape going westwards.

PSEUSTES

It was, I think, but smoke. Yet I am frightened.

SYCOPHANTES

Is it not further off?

PSEUSTES

Yes, it is further. [*More thunder.*]

SYCOPHANTES

That time it was fainter.

ALEXANDER ACT I

PSEUSTES

Yes, I am easier now.

SYCOPHANTES

The old man went that way.

PSEUSTES

Yes, he was going that way by the hills; he will have a fearful journey.

SYCOPHANTES

Well, he is gone now and the great storm with him. We are well rid of both.

PSEUSTES

Here's Alexander.

[*Enter* ALEXANDER.]

ALEXANDER

Well friends, what do you here?

SYCOPHANTES

We three were sheltering here.

ALEXANDER

Why, where's the third?

SYCOPHANTES

Indeed you know him not, O Alexander. The third was Fear. He came to us from the storm.

ACT I *ALEXANDER*

ALEXANDER [*looking afraid*]
Speak not of the storm. I forbid you to speak of it. There are things men should not speak of.

SYCOPHANTES
Indeed, Alexander, such a storm . . .

ALEXANDER
No, my friend, we will speak of other things.

SYCOPHANTES
Then we are silent. For of one thing only all men speak to-day, and of this we may not speak lest we be thought to praise you and I that flatter no man be called a flatterer.

ALEXANDER
A soldier needs no praises. What do you speak of?

SYCOPHANTES
Of your valour as a soldier we do not speak nor of your captain's skill, but all men say a new star shines on Asia, in Alexander's wisdom, which is such as none have known in the old time even.

ALEXANDER.
No, no, no, this is flattery.

SYCOPHANTES
Alexander, none have said this of me ever and gone unrebuked, and I have ever been an honest

man. Now that the wisest say I am but a flatterer I may hold up my head no more.

Alexander

I spoke hastily. Forget it.

Sycophantes

Never shall I forget it. I have been called a base thing not by some fool but by the wisest man that Asia knows. Never shall I hold up my head again.

Alexander

Come, come, I spoke in haste.

Sycophantes

No, though he speak in haste Alexander does not err, and yet I knew not I was a flatterer. I did no more than say what all men know, and knew not that the truth was flattery, being unskilled altogether in the flatterer's hateful ways.

Alexander

Yes, yes, you are no flatterer.

Sycophantes

No, for I speak nothing but the blunt truth always, after saying what the others durst not, and now I tell this plain tale that none have told you, knowing their danger if they speak of these things; but I speak of it because it is right that you should know. All Asia is terror-stricken,

ACT I   *ALEXANDER*

wondering at your wisdom, and none dare tell you this. Wherever you set foot throughout all Asia it is known to all that men will abandon their kings and be ruled by you for the sake of your famous wisdom, and none but I dare tell you.

Alexander
I fear you flatter me.

Sycophantes
I readily pay the penalty. Slay me for what I have said, because none else dare tell you. Slay me but take my message. Asia awaits you.

Alexander [*giving gold ornament*]
There, there, we shall not slay you.

Sycophantes
Thank you, great son of Philip.

Pseustes
He is not the son of Philip.

Alexander
What!

Pseustes
Son of God, it has long been said by all, no *man* could do what you have accomplished.

[*Bewildered silence falls on all, even on* Alexander.]

ALEXANDER

ALEXANDER
You say my mother played King Philip false?

PSEUSTES
Even for sacred Zeus.

ALEXANDER
Who says this?

PSEUSTES
Son of God, all men say it.

[*The* FLATTERERS *steal away one by one until* ALEXANDER *is left alone still deep in thought.*]

ALEXANDER [*solus*]
True. No man has done what I have done. And yet . . . Again Zeus is the father of all, but that is mere . . . And it were politic to be divine. [*He calls for* PRIEST. PRIEST *enters.*] You have heard what men are saying?

PRIEST
They say many things, O Alexander. They say . . .

ALEXANDER
They say that Zeus begat me. [*The* PRIEST *is silent.*] And what say you?

PRIEST
In all the affairs of men, O Alexander, there is doubt. Of their going hence there is doubt

ACT I   *ALEXANDER*

whither they go, and a greater doubt there is of their coming hither, in what manner they came.

ALEXANDER

But what say you who are wise in all these things?

PRIEST

Humility, O Alexander, is dearer to Zeus than wisdom. Shall I presume to speak of his goings forth or to know things that are hidden?

ALEXANDER

A crafty answer.

PRIEST

O Alexander, I am a simple man and unaccustomed to have speech with kings.

ALEXANDER

Answer me straightly. Give me no subtleties. Am I the son of Zeus?

PRIEST

You are the son of Zeus, the father of all.

ALEXANDER

You simple man, you have the cunning of Woman.

PRIEST

Pardon the ignorance of a poor plain man.

ALEXANDER [*rising*]

Your ignorance shall be instructed. Learn then that I am the son of Zeus, as many have said, and not the son of Philip, or of any mortal man. Learn that I am immortal like my father, whom Chronos begat in the old time: and in proof of this I will burn Persepolis, the city of such kings.

PRIEST

O Alexander, you would not burn Persepolis, so holy from ancient days. That is a frightful thought.

ALEXANDER

It is a frightful thought, and *I* have thought it. No mortal man durst think it.

THAIS [*who has sidled on*]

It was my thought, Alexander.

ALEXANDER

You err. I alone have thought it.

THAIS

It was my thought. I was drunk and I cried out burn Persepolis. It was my thought, Alexander.

ALEXANDER

Peace woman! What do you know of the thoughts of the sons of god? [*He looks at her and she goes withering away.*] Torch-bearers! Torch-

ACT I   *ALEXANDER*

bearers! [*Enter* TORCH-BEARERS.] Burn Persepolis.

[*Exeunt* TORCH-BEARERS; *they reappear at back, passing decoratively.* ALEXANDER *picks up a torch. Exit* ALEXANDER. *A glare is seen and increases. Persepolis burns.*]

PRIEST [*kneeling down, facing the burning*]

O gods of Persepolis, gods of Persepolis: I know ye cannot avail against Alexander: yet make one little curse before you burn. One little curse. Let him one day be even as this [*pointing at fallen Xerxes*].

[*The gods blaze.*]

Curtain

ACT II

SCENE I

Scene: Beyond Persia.

ALEXANDER *is no longer a simple soldier but is dressed in Persian silks.*

[*Enter* NEARCHOS.]

NEARCHOS
You sent for me, Alexander.

ALEXANDER
I looked last night upon the silver stars,

NEARCHOS
Upon the stars, Alexander?

ALEXANDER
I am no longer what I was, Nearchos.

NEARCHOS
No, Alexander.

ALEXANDER
There was a time when every battle won, when every new horizon of the earth was joy and triumph. Now I have seen the stars.

ACT II *ALEXANDER*

NEARCHOS

The stars, Alexander?

ALEXANDER

I have looked long on them. They are so many: great multitudes that rise and wheel and set and know not Alexander.

NEARCHOS

They are only stars.

ALEXANDER

I cared not once: now I am different. I am greater; but not happier, Nearchos.

NEARCHOS

Happiness goes with the Greek dress and the Greek ways.

ALEXANDER

So it was once.

NEARCHOS

And now?

ALEXANDER

Now the world mocks me with all its hills and peoples, saying, "We are not conquered." But I *will* conquer them. I will take the world to the uttermost: all its lands shall be mine, and I will look with ease on the contemptuous stars. Therefore go you, Nearchos, with all your ships

into the farthest gulfs. See India; mark it well.
Search out the seas, even to Oceanus, beyond
which there is nothing. Mark Æthiopia; learn
the lie of it. Look for the kingdom that men call
Cathay, that garden country with its fabulous
wall. If there be such a land bring word of it.
And to all kingdoms to whose shores you sail say
"Alexander comes."

Nearchos

I go, Alexander. Wear Persian silks, dismiss
wise councillors, turn even from the gods; only
be Alexander, and you have my fealty, my sword,
and my bended knee.

Alexander

I know, Nearchos.

Nearchos

I'll toil for you, I'll sail the seas of the world,
I'll fight for you. The grey hairs have come upon
my head, but I'll work on. When they send us
such a man as Alexander what else would we do
—though he dress like a Persian and forget the
Greeks?

Alexander

He will come no more, whom I have sent away;
he is gone, Nearchos. And sometimes now I
forget what is due to the Greeks. Yet will I
remember; I do not need his counsel, I will remember. I will send for Clitus. *There* is a Greek,
there is a Macedonian. I will send for Clitus.

SCENE I *ALEXANDER*

Why, I have not seen Clitus for many days. I will see Clitus and so remember again the ways of Greece. Ho! Send hither Clitus, Ptolemy too and Perdiccas. [*To* NEARCHOS.] I will be with Greeks and recover that austere spirit that Hellas gave me.

[*Exit* SENTRY.]

NEARCHOS

Right or wrong, Greek dress or Persian, my sword is for Alexander.

ALEXANDER

Nearchos, if I were a husbandman with a small cottage on the hills of Greece, with a field to be tilled with labour, would you have worked with me?

NEARCHOS

Yes, Alexander.

ALEXANDER [*sighs*]

I have chosen the world instead, with Oceanus for my boundary. Haply a small field with a rustic hedge, and such a friend as you, were happier. Well, I have chosen and the dice are cast, the gods have read the numbers. Farewell, Nearchos.

NEARCHOS

Farewell, my liege lord.

[*Exit* NEARCHOS.]

ALEXANDER

So he is gone. Be humbled, Alexander, that have, beyond the deserts of any man, so loyal a servant. Yet am I not the son of a sacred Zeus? No, I will not be humbled, that were not fitting.
[*Enter* PTOLEMY *and* PERDICCAS.]
Ptolemy, greeting. Greeting, Perdiccas.

PTOLEMY AND PERDICCAS

Greeting, Alexander.

ALEXANDER

Well, Ptolemy, the world is still unconquered. But I have sent Nearchos down its coasts to search it out. Then we will conquer it all.

PERDICCAS

All? 'Tis a large world, Alexander.

ALEXANDER

A large world, yes. And full of little men. Have larger dreams, Perdiccas. The world's small enough. There's room for many of them in my dreams.

PTOLEMY

Many *worlds?*

ALEXANDER

Yes, *many* worlds. And were there more, why, I would conquer more. Such is your leader.

SCENE I *ALEXANDER*

But let us plan. We are so far into the land of Persia that the next kingdom for me should be India.

PTOLEMY [*to* PERDICCAS]

India.

ALEXANDER

Well, we'll take India. Then we'll await Nearchos, and hear if there be a kingdom of Cathay and learn the lie of Æthiopia, whether Oceanus cuts off its coast, as the gods ordain for every other land, or whether she lifts her terrible, barren head out to the stars.

PTOLEMY

How shall Nearchos find you?

ALEXANDER

How find Alexander? Be guided by bloody fields, by blazing towns and broken armaments, or ask the way of wandering exiled kings. Find Alexander!

[*Enter* CLITUS *with* THAIS.]

Why, Clitus!

CLITUS

Hail!

ALEXANDER

My Clitus. I have not seen you these many days.

ALEXANDER ACT II

CLITUS

There have been so many Persians all about you that one could not push through the throng to come to you.

ALEXANDER

Ah, Clitus, I will put off the Persian dress. I will be Greek again. [*Casts his wreath away.*] But since he left me, he of whom we spake, I have been somewhat different. Ah, Clitus, you advised me ill that day we burnt Persepolis.

CLITUS [*gravely*]

I advised you ill.

ALEXANDER

Yet I'll be Greek again.

CLITUS

Pray that old man that he return, Alexander.

THAIS

No, Clitus.

ALEXANDER

No, he is gone, and will not come again; nor is it fitting; I will not bend my will for gods or men.

CLITUS

Ah, we were terribly mistaken.

SCENE I   *ALEXANDER*

ALEXANDER
Say not we were mistaken, my dear Clitus, for you forget that I being the son of Zeus have not the power to err.

CLITUS
Alexander the son of Zeus!

ALEXANDER
Even so my Clitus, and none the less your very dearest friend though you are mortal.

CLITUS
The son of Zeus. I never heard anything so ridiculous.

ALEXANDER
Clitus!! Clitus, you are my friend, and your foolish words are forgiven as soon as uttered. Why, I forget them. Yet consider, Clitus, many a man had died for saying what you said. I know you did not mean it. But we of the holy line bear insults badly.

CLITUS
Insults. I did not insult you. You talked nonsense and I said so. You are talking nonsense now. I do not mind you talking it, Alexander.

THAIS
Be silent, Clitus.

ALEXANDER

Clitus, no other man on earth had said so much and lived.

CLITUS

I will not be silent, Thais. Alexander says he is the son of Zeus.

PERDICCAS

He is the undoubted son of sacred Zeus.

CLITUS

And now Perdiccas is talking nonsense, Thais.

PTOLEMY

Clitus, none doubt he is the son of Zeus.

CLITUS

And now Ptolemy.

THAIS

Be silent, fool.

ALEXANDER

Clitus, you shall die.

[THAIS *runs up to* ALEXANDER *and abstracts his sword. Exit* THAIS.]

THAIS [*as she goes, to* PERDICCAS *and* PTOLEMY] Lead him away.

ALEXANDER

Give me my sword!

SCENE I   *ALEXANDER*

CLITUS

Do not be silly, Alexander. I only said that Ptolemy talked nonsense when he called you the son of Zeus. You're the son of Philip of Macedon. Isn't that enough?

ALEXANDER

Sound the alarm. Sound the alarm, I say. This is treason.

[SENTRY *at first disobeys, then raises his bugle. Enter* THAIS.]

THAIS

Do not sound it. There'll be an uproar in the camp if you touch that. Lead him out, he's crazy.

[PERDICCAS *and* PTOLEMY *pull* CLITUS *out.*]

CLITUS [*going*]

Crazy? I only said . . . [*Exit.*]

[PERDICCAS *and* PTOLEMY *return to soothe* ALEXANDER; *re-enter* CLITUS *by another door.*]

CLITUS

Thais, I'm not crazy. Why do you say I'm crazy?

ALEXANDER

Give me a sword. You die for this treason, Clitus.

ALEXANDER ACT II

THAIS

There are no swords here. He is mad, Alexander. He's mad. We all know you're the son of Zeus.

CLITUS

I'm not mad. I say his mother is an honest woman, he says . . .

[ALEXANDER, *snatching a javelin suddenly from a soldier who enters, rushes towards* CLITUS. CLITUS *stands still, then he realizes and flies.* ALEXANDER *pursues him off.* PERDICCAS *and* PTOLEMY *follow to doorway, but are too late. Re-enter* ALEXANDER.]

ALEXANDER

I have killed him. I've killed Clitus. Clitus, I did not mean it! I . . . Clitus, meet me when you come from school by the big oak tree on the hill and we'll go down the valley hunting again together. . . . It cannot be that he is dead. For if he's dead we cannot hunt again, and he and I are going hunting this evening when Clitus comes from school.

PERDICCAS [*to* PTOLEMY]

Yes, he's quite dead.

ALEXANDER

"Dead," someone says. Not Clitus. But he's not dead in my dreams. Let us see. Come not near me; I will think. Which are real, my

SCENE I *ALEXANDER*

dreams or this hard world? I see this place. Now there are tears in my eyes, and I see Clitus hunting on the hills upon a summer's evening. Surely he is not dead.

PTOLEMY

Clitus is quite dead.

ALEXANDER

Dead!

PTOLEMY

We cannot pull the javelin from his body.

ALEXANDER

The javelin? Ah! Where is it?

[*He rushes to exit and is stopped by* PTOLEMY, PERDICCAS, *and* THAIS.]

THEY

No.

ALEXANDER [*returning to centre, sitting down, weeping.*]

They will not let me die. They will not let me die. It is only a little thing I would ask of them, and I am Alexander. Thais, dear Thais, give me a little thing, give me a little dagger, a small jewelled dagger, I ask no more than this of you, Thais.

[THAIS *weeps and does not hear.*]

PTOLEMY
No, Alexander.

ALEXANDER
Thais, Thais.

PTOLEMY
She cannot hear you.   She loved Clitus.
[ALEXANDER *sinks to the floor.*]
[*To* PERDICCAS.]
I do not think he will seek to kill himself now. Yet we will take the javelin from the body, and let no weapon be brought near him.

PERDICCAS
Will this fit pass away?

PTOLEMY
I think it will pass now.

PERDICCAS
What a frightful spirit he has. It is swift as a bird, strong as a lion; now to do this, now to do that.
[ALEXANDER *moans.*]
He is crying out against it now.   What can a man do against his spirit?

PTOLEMY
Poor Clitus.

SCENE I *ALEXANDER*

PERDICCAS

Ah. Yet we are somewhat nearer Alexander, you and I, now he's dead.

PTOLEMY

Why, that may be.

PERDICCAS

And something greater, Ptolemy.

PTOLEMY

Yet I would have him back if there were a path back.

[THAIS *mutters.*]

What does she say?

THAIS

Oh—h.

PTOLEMY

Take comfort, Thais. Weep not my pretty Thais. You must not spoil your beautiful face with tears.

THAIS

I loved Clitus.

PTOLEMY

We all love you, Thais, and your little childish ways. Do not weep.

THAIS

I loved Clitus. I have had many lovers. I loved Clitus last. None more shall love me. I will paint my face no more. I am an old, old woman.

PERDICCAS [*to* PTOLEMY]

She does not know what she is saying.

[THAIS *goes off sobbing.*]

PTOLEMY [*to* PERDICCAS]

Come, leave him awhile. We will set an unarmed guard about this place so that he do not slay himself. Come hence.

[*Exeunt.*]

[ALEXANDER *is left alone prostrate.*]

Curtain

(*Three days elapse*)

ACT II

Scene II

ALEXANDER *lies on the floor moaning of* CLITUS.

A PHYSICIAN
Speak to him of his country.

ATTENDANT
He raves and none may speak with him.

PHYSICIAN
Give him to drink of the wine of some Macedonian vineyard growing by hills he knew.

ATTENDANT
He will not drink, nor eat, nor sleep, but only moans for Clitus.

PHYSICIAN
What is that?

ATTENDANT
It is the dancing women that we sent for to dance to him; it may be that when he sees the women dance . . .

Physician

Yes. Let us come away.

[*Exeunt.*]

[*Enter the* Dancing Women, *they dance past him.*]

Alexander

Ah. You have not heard that Clitus is dead. [*They go on dancing.*] I tell you Clitus is dead. [*They go on dancing.*] What! You would dance when he is dead? When sweet young Clitus is dead and none should dance again? Away! Away! Away! [*They flee.*]

[*Enter* Attendant.]

Attendant

Alexander. Alexander. There are come across the desert all manner of terrible men from the barbarous countries. We bade them stop, but they would not heed us and came on, each tribe of barbarians racing against the other. [Alexander *takes no heed.*] They are all here, now; from Araby, from the mountains, and I know not from where else. [Alexander *lies silent.*] Terrible men, Alexander, have come. They are here now.

[*Exit in despair.*]

[*Enter the* Ambassador of the Nomads. *He has horned headgear.*]

SCENE II   *ALEXANDER*

AMBASSADOR OF NOMADS

I am first. Where's Alexander? [*He walks up to the prostrate* ALEXANDER.] Where's Alexander?

ALEXANDER

What?

AMBASSADOR OF NOMADS

Quick. I must see him. [*Looks over shoulder.*] Where's Alexander?

ALEXANDER

Why, I'm Alexander. [*Sits up, leaning on one arm.*]

[AMBASSADOR OF NOMADS *takes a step back and prostrates himself.* ALEXANDER *still looking at him. The retinue of the Nomads prostrate themselves also.*]

AMBASSADOR OF NOMADS

O Alexander, we be the Nomad people, and if you will deign to make a treaty with us we will give you the quarter of our herds, as well as a thousand of our huge-headed spears, and cunning bowmen who shall fight for you, and a hundred of those swift, notable horses that we get from the plains; only make a treaty with us.

ALEXANDER

Have you killed your friend? Have you ever slain your companion?

ALEXANDER   ACT II

Ambassador of Nomads
Why no. Not my friend.

Alexander
Then I will make no treaty with you nor speak with you, for there is only one thing that I wish to speak of.

Ambassador of Nomads
If you will make a treaty, O Alexander, we will give you *half* our herds, as well as our huge-headed spears, the bowmen and the swift horses.

Alexander
I will not speak of treaties when Clitus is dead. For he is lying in that chamber now with a white coverlet upon his body, and he is dead. We must not speak of any other thing.

Ambassador of Nomads [*stepping back*]
Alexander! Is this Alexander! Is it Alexander whom the nations tremble at? Alexander!

Alexander
Yes, it is I. I killed Clitus.

[*Enter the* Ambassador of the Hill-men *with retinue. They have huge sheepskins and great knives, etc.*]

[*Enter hastily the* Ambassador of the Arabs *with retinue; each man has several swords and long knives in his belt.*]

SCENE II   *ALEXANDER*

AMBASSADOR OF NOMADS [*scornfully*]
Make your treaty with Alexander.
[*He gathers his men with a sign of his hand. Exeunt all the Nomads.*]
[AMBASSADOR OF THE HILL-MEN *when he sees it is* ALEXANDER *kneels down with all his men.*]

AMBASSADOR OF HILL-MEN

O Alexander, make with *us* a treaty. Make your treaty with us, Alexander. None can bring you such tribute as we can bring, for it is all secret what the hills possess. It is all secret, none knows what it is, none knows the place of it. But listen, Alexander, you do not hear me. I speak of the secret of the hills. We will bring you amethysts from the precipices, which we get with the long rope of Asjar; there is no way to get them but by dangling down, and no other rope so long; we keep it at Asjar in our brazen house. But hear me, Alexander. We will give you the gold that the cataract brings down, old Hill-Thunder our cataract, that no man has ever seen but the men of the hills. The gold comes down at morning and flattens with the fall, and the crags that it comes from are unknown to man, even the mountaineers. And opals also from the high hills of snow. But —you do not hear me. I speak of the secret of the holy hills—and you do not hear.

ALEXANDER

Have you killed your friend? Your dearest friend, have you slain him?

ALEXANDER ACT II

AMBASSADOR OF HILL-MEN
Why—that is not the custom of the hill-men.

ALEXANDER
Then I will not speak with you.

AMBASSADOR OF HILL-MEN
Is it not beautiful to speak of the hills?

ALEXANDER
I say I will not.

AMBASSADOR OF HILL-MEN [*walking slowly away backwards*]
You should have had our treasure and known the ancient secret of the hills.

ALEXANDER
I will not speak with you.

AMBASSADOR OF THE ARABS
O Alexander, we also would make a treaty.

ALEXANDER
I make no treaties. It is not a time for treaties. For what purpose should you need a treaty? I will not speak of it.

AMBASSADOR OF THE ARABS
Hear me, Alexander.

SCENE II *ALEXANDER*

ALEXANDER

Have you slain your companion that I should speak with you, and have you killed your friend?

AMBASSADOR OF THE ARABS

Yes, Alexander.

ALEXANDER [*rising*]

You have slain your friend?

AMBASSADOR OF THE ARABS [*departing*]

Yes, Alexander.

ALEXANDER

Stay! Stay! I would speak with you. Do not leave me. Yes, we will speak together. We will speak long, you and I.

[ALEXANDER *rises, goes up to* AMBASSADOR OF THE ARABS, *and puts his arm round his shoulders.*]

So you slew your friend.

AMBASSADOR OF THE ARABS

Why. Yes, Alexander.

ALEXANDER

Are we not in the dark place, you and I? Verily in the dark midmost place of the world's sorrows. Was it long ago? But what has time to do with it, our sorrow is a twin immortal cypress, it neither fades nor grows. For me the gods planted it three days ago.

ALEXANDER

Ambassador of the Arabs

Ah, doubtless.

Alexander

What? But you do not speak. I, too, am silent sometimes for many hours, sometimes I rave. I know not which is better. Is it better, think you, to rave?

Ambassador of the Arabs

Perhaps the council chamber and the making of treaties best turns one's mind away.

Alexander

We must not speak of treaties, you and I. They do not know our sorrow, they that speak of treaties. They do not know. But let us speak of Clitus.

Ambassador of the Arabs

Yes, yes, we will speak of Clitus first, and after that then . . .

Alexander

Why yes, of your dear friend. But we will speak of him first. Indeed I will not be selfish in my sorrow. We are the world's most chosen, you and I. The two to whom the gods have given the first of sorrows. What was his name?

Ambassador of the Arabs

His name? Ah, yes, my friend's: his name was Nasrāeel.

SCENE II   *ALEXANDER*

ALEXANDER
And what befell? You quarrelled?

AMBASSADOR OF THE ARABS
Why yes, we quarrelled.

ALEXANDER
And upon what matter?

AMBASSADOR OF THE ARABS
Upon the matter of . . . it was at a banquet.

ALEXANDER
Yes? yes?

AMBASSADOR OF THE ARABS
We had drunk wine. I said a certain woman of Ind was beautiful. Maharb said a certain woman of Persia was lovelier.

ALEXANDER
Maharb?

AMBASSADOR OF THE ARABS
Yes. My friend.

ALEXANDER
But your friend was Nasrāeel.

AMBASSADOR OF THE ARABS
I called him Maharb.

ALEXANDER
Yes. Yes. And then?

AMBASSADOR OF THE ARABS
Why then I slew him.

ALEXANDER
You slew him, and with what weapon?

AMBASSADOR OF THE ARABS
Why, with my sword.

ALEXANDER
I will tell you a dreadful thing. I will tell you for we are the twins of sorrow. I killed Clitus with a horrible javelin.

AMBASSADOR OF THE ARABS
Indeed, O Alexander, we are the twins of sorrow. Let us, therefore, make a treaty, you and I, that we may proclaim our brotherhood.

ALEXANDER
Let us rather speak of the dreadful things we have done, and how we became the heirs of an equal doom. Tell me how Nasrāeel looked when he was dead. Did he speak as you killed him?

AMBASSADOR OF THE ARABS
No, he did not speak.

ALEXANDER
Clitus tried to speak. I think he would have spoken.

SCENE II *ALEXANDER*

AMBASSADOR OF THE ARABS

Nasrāeel did not speak.

ALEXANDER

Tell me more.

AMBASSADOR OF THE ARABS

We buried Nasrāeel.

ALEXANDER

And then? Used you to sleep? Or did you lie awake with terrible dreams? How many nights is it before sleep comes?

AMBASSADOR OF THE ARABS

Why, I do not remember. I busied myself about the affairs of my country. I made treaties with other countries and so I forgot my grief.

ALEXANDER

You forgot?

AMBASSADOR OF THE ARABS

Yes, I made treaties: there is no other thing that so soon drowns remembrance.

ALEXANDER

Is that so?

AMBASSADOR OF THE ARABS

Yes, treaties——

ALEXANDER

But we must not speak of treaties. Come, and I will tell you of Clitus. Clitus and I were as two hounds chasing one hare together, so together we sought glory. We were as fire and light, song and echo. Clitus and I were of the one country; knew the same hills; held the same valleys and small rivers holy, remembered the same old tales. O Arab, I killed Clitus, and he is dead.

AMBASSADOR OF THE ARABS

It is most sad, and we will mourn for Clitus, when you deign to grant the treaty that we seek.

ALEXANDER

Clitus was young, Clitus was fair, and nimble, Clitus was ever . . . but I perceive you do not hear me.

AMBASSADOR OF THE ARABS

Indeed I hear you . . . but this treaty.

ALEXANDER

No more of treaties. Is not Clitus dead?

AMBASSADOR OF THE ARABS [*with a high motion of his hand to his men*]

It is useless. Come.

[*Exeunt.*]

[ALEXANDER *sinks to the floor again. Enter with retinue the* QUEEN OF THE AMAZONS.]

SCENE II   *ALEXANDER*

QUEEN OF THE AMAZONS
I come to challenge to combat Alexander.

ALEXANDER [*looking up from the floor*]
Why, I am Alexander.

QUEEN OF THE AMAZONS
You Alexander that overthrew Darius?

ALEXANDER
I am Alexander that killed Clitus.

QUEEN OF THE AMAZONS [*saluting with her sword*]
I am a Queen and leader of Amazons, and am come to challenge to combat Alexander.

ALEXANDER
Alas for Clitus.

QUEEN OF THE AMAZONS
Is it seemly that one so well spoken of as you are by those that walk upon the fields of war should lie thus without his sword?

ALEXANDER
Clitus is dead.

QUEEN OF THE AMAZONS
Will you do combat with me or make battle against the Amazons? [ALEXANDER *bursts into tears.*] But a grief has come upon you and you are in trouble. [*She runs up to him as he writhes*

on to his back. She goes on one knee and takes his head on her lap.] Rest your head, it aches. [*She puts her hand on his forehead.*] Trouble is terrible, but all things pass like the water from the hills. It will not always be like this. Rest your head. What was it? What was it?

ALEXANDER

I killed Clitus.

QUEEN OF THE AMAZONS

And Clitus was your friend, a dear friend, and you were angry? Yes, that is terrible. But you will be better soon. That is always so when it is violent at first. It will pass away, all things pass.

ALEXANDER

Clitus is dead.

QUEEN OF THE AMAZONS

Do not weep for Clitus. There are no troubles in death. You must not weep for Clitus, it is only life that has troubles. I am often in trouble, but we must bear with life as well as we may. Only the dead are safe.

ALEXANDER

Have you killed your companion, have you ever slain your sister?

QUEEN OF THE AMAZONS

I had a dear friend once when we were children. We quarrelled once and I slapped her in the face.

SCENE II   *ALEXANDER*

It was many years ago and we were children. But year in, year out, whenever the Spring comes round (it was in Spring that I did it), when the oleander buds break into blossom, I remember this and weep, though it is so long since and we were children.

ALEXANDER

You have never slain a man.

QUEEN OF THE AMAZONS

Do not stir. Rest your head. I have slain many men. Yet I weep whenever the oleander blossoms.

ALEXANDER

Comfort me not unless you bring back Clitus.

QUEEN OF THE AMAZONS

Have you slept?

ALEXANDER

Not for three nights. [*A pause, she strokes his forehead.*] Comfort me not who cannot bring back Clitus. [*A pause, still stroking his head.*] How can I forget, how can I forget for ever? Tell me how I may forget Clitus.

QUEEN OF THE AMAZONS

Life is violent and full of sorrow. We must tire it, and when it is over we must rest.

ALEXANDER

ALEXANDER
How may I tire life?

QUEEN OF THE AMAZONS
By the practice of the art.

ALEXANDER
What art should I practise? Ah! but I cannot forget. Clitus, Clitus, Clitus, I may not forget you.

QUEEN OF THE AMAZONS
There is only one art that is worthy of life.

ALEXANDER
What art can weary life into forgetfulness and bring rest soon?

QUEEN OF THE AMAZONS
The lovely art of war.

ALEXANDER
Ah! [*A pause.*] I am very weary.

QUEEN OF THE AMAZONS
Rest, Alexander.
[*He falls asleep, head still on her knee. Somebody enters, she raises her hand for silence. He tiptoes off to others in the door.*]

ONE
He sleeps.

SCENE II   *ALEXANDER*

ANOTHER

Then he will live.

ANOTHER

He sleeps.

[*Exeunt softly.* ALEXANDER *and the* QUEEN OF THE AMAZONS *remain quite still. Suddenly he starts up half sitting, half reclining on one arm. She rises.*]

ALEXANDER

Ha. I have dreamed of India. Ah, Clitus is dead. But you should have seen India as I dreamed it. There were elephants with rams upon their foreheads, cavalry with white horses, kings with scimitars, camels laden with turquoises from the mountains, and kingdoms to be had for the taking.

QUEEN OF THE AMAZONS

Go and take those kingdoms, Alexander, there is no good art but war.

ALEXANDER

What a wife for Alexander.

QUEEN OF THE AMAZONS

I am a soldier and give my hand to no man.

ALEXANDER

Then—you will never have children to comfort when they weep.

QUEEN OF THE AMAZONS

Oh yes, for strange and difficult are the chances of war. Some day there may come a conqueror?

ALEXANDER

Do you fear you will ever be conquered?

QUEEN OF THE AMAZONS

It will come one day from the left flank. The flanks are ever most vulnerable. My picked women march on the right flank.

ALEXANDER

And you would wed a conqueror?

QUEEN OF THE AMAZONS

That is as it pleases the victor.

ALEXANDER

It would be a terrible thing for one so like the dawn over the plains, or like the little winds that run free in the morning to endure servitude.

QUEEN OF THE AMAZONS

What matter how marriage comes, marriage that brings obedience and all the cares of a house.

ALEXANDER

And you would forget the noble art of war?

SCENE II   *ALEXANDER*

QUEEN OF THE AMAZONS

I would forget it all, and the bright raids in the morning.

ALEXANDER

I will be that conqueror.

QUEEN OF THE AMAZONS

That is as must be decided on some cornfield as yet untrodden by soldiers, or on hungry plains of grass that have not yet tasted blood.

ALEXANDER

What do they name you?

QUEEN OF THE AMAZONS

They name me Rhododactilos.

ALEXANDER

A fair name and a terrible. I will put aside my grief and conquer the world even to India. Thence I will bring the nations against your gates for war, O Rhododactilos.

QUEEN OF THE AMAZONS

It is a noble art.

ALEXANDER

How well was it said of the sword that it is the founder of cities.

ALEXANDER

QUEEN OF THE AMAZONS
It was well said.

ALEXANDER
And yet of what avail is it if the sword overturn them again? Can your wisdom answer me this hard question?

QUEEN OF THE AMAZONS
It is no hard question to one that is versed in the art of war, for man takes after his mother and is even like to the earth, which needs must be broken and turned, and broken and turned again, or ever it bring to birth the golden corn. So man and his cities must be broken with war to bring forth his wisdom and strength. The sword is the ploughshare of man, that he grow not corrupt in his cities.

ALEXANDER
Well said, O Queen Rhododactilos. We will make a mighty warfare, you and I, on my way from the ends of the world.

QUEEN OF THE AMAZONS
Even so, Alexander.

ALEXANDER
O Queen, I would not that you came to harm. Fight not against my men of Macedon; but, sitting aloof in your palace, send forth your Captains.

SCENE II *ALEXANDER*

QUEEN OF THE AMAZONS
It was ever my wont to lead my Amazons.

ALEXANDER
No, no, Queen; go not forth. My men of Macedon are swift and mighty.

QUEEN OF THE AMAZONS
I ever lead my Amazons.

ALEXANDER
But if you are killed, my poor Queen Rhododactilos?

QUEEN OF THE AMAZONS
Many women die. But if you are killed, Alexander?

ALEXANDER
I am immortal.

QUEEN OF THE AMAZONS
Indeed some have said so.

ALEXANDER
You do not believe then that I am immortal?

QUEEN OF THE AMAZONS
No, Alexander, *I have seen the immortals.* I saw them once upon my hills at evening. I know the calm look of their marble faces. Their cold

ALEXANDER ACT II

eyes chilled the evening. Among them are never tears and never laughter.

ALEXANDER

Let Mars decide. I may be long in India, and at the end of the world where the earth runs down to Oceanus; but one day I shall come with my Macedonians, though you had twenty armies.

QUEEN OF THE AMAZONS

My Amazons shall watch for you in the passes.

ALEXANDER

We shall meet then over your broken ramparts.

QUEEN OF THE AMAZONS

We shall meet face to face on fields of war.

ALEXANDER

Never looked lovers to so strange a meeting.

QUEEN OF THE AMAZONS

I love no man.

ALEXANDER

If you could have loved a man, might it have been Alexander?

QUEEN OF THE AMAZONS

How can I say who am free, or how know who have never been conquered?

SCENE II *ALEXANDER*

ALEXANDER
But how if I should conquer you with my men of Macedon behind me?

QUEEN OF THE AMAZONS
If I were vanquished there were no more to say.

ALEXANDER
Men say that I was magnanimous at Issus.

QUEEN OF THE AMAZONS
I have no need of magnanimity. Let me have the favour of God and the fair chances of war.

ALEXANDER
To what god do you look?

QUEEN OF THE AMAZONS
I know no god but Mars.
[*She goes to the door.*]

ALEXANDER
Farewell till we meet in battle, Queen of the Amazons.

QUEEN OF THE AMAZONS
Farewell, Alexander.

ALEXANDER
Farewell, wonderful soldier.

QUEEN OF THE AMAZONS

O Alexander, when you make war on me go up against me with horses.

ALEXANDER

Why with horses?

QUEEN OF THE AMAZONS

Because we—because my women have seldom stood against horses. Against infantry we are invincible.

ALEXANDER

O Rhododactilos.

QUEEN OF THE AMAZONS

Farewell, Alexander.

ALEXANDER

I will come with elephants out of India and most swift horses.

[*Exit* QUEEN OF THE AMAZONS.]

ALEXANDER

What a mother for heroes. . . . But Clitus is dead. . . . What was it he said? He said my father was Philip of Macedon. And so I killed him. Such is man. Such is man, and I had thought to be greater than the gods. O Clitus, Apollo hath taken you thus terribly, using my own mad hands. [*He looks at his hands.*]

[*Enter the* PRIEST OF APOLLO.]

SCENE II   *ALEXANDER*

PRIEST OF APOLLO

Be humbled now and turn to the god again, and seek peace of Apollo.

ALEXANDER

Humbled? Apollo? No! He hath done this to me; let him do even more. But what god or beast or man shall humble Alexander? Nay, I will overrun his India and sack that torrid Asia that he loves.

PRIEST OF APOLLO

What can a man avail against a god?

ALEXANDER

Let us put it to the test. Let him save India.

PRIEST OF APOLLO

It is written that he is terrible over India.

ALEXANDER

Then to India.

[HERALDS *take up the cry. The trumpets of the legions are heard one by one.*]

Curtain

ACT III

Scene I

A ruined temple in Gedrosia on the way back from India. There are carven gods against the wall. The roof is gone.

ALEXANDER [*wreathed in roses*]
Have we not rioted?

A RHETORICIAN
I have for my theme the virtues of Alexander.

SYCOPHANTES
What nobler theme could any man desire?

RHETORICIAN
It is neither seemly nor is it the wish of Alexander himself that others should speak while I orate.

SYCOPHANTES
I but praised your theme.

RHETORICIAN
It is not a theme for a man to speak of idly. My theme is the virtues . . .

ACT III *ALEXANDER*

SYCOPHANTES

I did not speak idly of . . .

RHETORICIAN

Hush—The virtues of Alexander. Of his valour and magnanimity I have spoken in my oration delivered in Persepolis, but of his temperance what bard shall sing, or what man praise it enough? It was the wonder of India. He was frugal even among wines so rare that the Indian dynasties that hoarded them had bought them drop by drop with royal pearls. His strength is such that they durst not go up against him with horses, but came with Behemoth, the elephant, and were utterly cast down, mountainous beast and man, by the power of Alexander.

He endured famine in deserts day after day and night-long hunger, and marched with only a little maize, and was not gluttonous in the granaries of kings, nor was he tempted with their age-old wine that they had bought drop by drop with royal pearls.

A YOUNG PUPIL [*plucking him by the sleeve*]

Master, you have said that already.

A RHETORICIAN

Ah yes, the pearls. Do not interrupt me. Should not such great forbearance be recorded more than twice? . . . with royal pearls. I say that he has endured hunger and been untempted with wine and has met Behemoth in the day of his anger face to face, even Behemoth the horrible monster of Asia, and has overcome him in war. He has come up like a lion out of Greece, and like the sun from the hills of Macedon. Kings have gone down before him and their crowns rolled away, and more kings came up against him; and always they brought Behemoth, who danced in his anger, and yet they could not prevail.

He is out upon the world like the North wind in winter, like Boreas in his youth; he is down upon Asia like the avalanche from the high hills of snow. Not all the maidens of Asia—a moment—In the warmth of the looks and longing of the fairest maidens of Asia his austere chastity was like those crags of ice that glitter and will not melt for any sun, floating as some have said in boreal seas.

ALEXANDER

This man wearies me. Somebody sing me a song about a goat.

DYONIS

I have a song about the god Pan himself, but it is not fit to be sung before so many.

ALEXANDER

What concerns Pan is fit to be sung before all mankind. Indeed his doings are most honourable. I shall bid my writers put together a book concerning them, I shall call it the Deeds of Pan.

DYONIS

O Pan, O Pan, O Pan—O˙ Pan—O Pan—O Pan, O Pan, O—[*He thinks deeply. Somebody suggests the word Pan.*] The very word [*musically*] O Pan.

SCENE I   *ALEXANDER*

ALEXANDER

Is there any more of this pleasant song?

DYONIS

O Alexander, there is much more, but I have forgotten it with many other beautiful things that happened long, long ago. When I think of the beautiful things I have forgotten I—weep. [*He weeps.*]

ALEXANDER [*rising and making obeisance to him*]

I make obeisance unto the god Bacchus who is indeed most manifest in you.

DYONIS

I am not worthy of this, your Grace, not worthy, not worthy.

ALEXANDER

I have noticed that the god Bacchus does not always choose the most worthy persons in whom to make himself manifest. Indeed, I have known worthy men unto whom Bacchus has never appeared at all, whereby those worthy men suffered much loss.

DYONIS

Without doubt, Alexander.

ALEXANDER

Bacchus is somewhat like a dog, he lies down in dirty places. He seems quite happy now to be rolling in thy nasty wits.

[COURTIERS *laugh at Dyonis.*]

Dyonis

Indeed, but I am sober.

Alexander

Sober, did anyone say sober? Search out and see whether anyone present be sober. Due reverence shall be paid to-day to Bacchus who has made himself manifest in the person of this Dyonis. I will have none sober when the god Bacchus deigns thus to manifest himself. Honour to Bacchus. If any man be found sober, let him be brought before me.

All

Honour to Bacchus.

Two Men [*pointing each a finger at the other with intense gravity, solemnly*]

Thou art sober.

[*They fall forward very, very slowly into each other's arms, thence to the ground, and move no more for the remainder of the act.*]

[*A man goes up to the stone statue of some god against the wall—loq.*]

I see two men that seem sober here.

Alexander

Bring them before me that I may try their heresy. [*The man tries to.*] Why do you not bring before me for judgment those heretics from the high grace of Bacchus?

SCENE I   *ALEXANDER*

Dyonis

O Alexander, one of them is so stubborn, dull and stony a heretic, that he stands like a whole phalanx, and the other is so nimble and airy that he eludes my grasp and may in no wise be handled.

Ptolemy

I cannot clearly see, your Grace, but I think he has hold of a god.

Alexander

Verily a god has hold of him, even most puissant Bacchus.

Dyonis [*struggling with the idol and clutching at its imagined duplicate*]

I can bring neither of them.

Alexander

It is indeed a most perplexing matter, nor can I discern its meaning, that when drunk we see two objects, whereas there be only one.

Perdiccas

Your Grace, it is indeed most wonderful.

Ptolemy

There is no answer to it among men.

Alexander

We will go into this matter thoroughly and sift it. I, Alexander, would know the wherefor of it. Bring hither Apoctes to me.

ALEXANDER

ACT III

Courtiers
Apoctes, O Apoctes. [*He comes.*]

Alexander
O Apoctes, most wise among the philosophers that honour Macedon, most wise, and yet I perceive thou art not drunk—there is no wisdom in not paying honour to Bacchus, so excellent a god —most wise, as I was saying, among the Greeks, and therefore most wise among the philosophers of the world—which I have conquered—What did I wish to say to Apoctes?

Perdiccas
O Alexander, thou didst wish to know the truth concerning this wonderful matter of seeing two men when there be only one.

Alexander
Indeed, it was so. A nice and difficult matter and one well worthy the wisdom of a philosopher. O Apoctes, most wise Apoctes, tell me concerning this difficult matter, even the matter of—of——

Perdiccas
Of seeing as two what is verily only one.

Alexander
Of seeing two when there is verily only one as this most learned Perdiccas has so well said, himself well honouring Bacchus.

SCENE I   *ALEXANDER*

APOCTES

O Alexander, this matter that thou hast set before me is one well worthy of the researches of so wise a king. Know then, O Alexander, that there be gods and gods, each having his proper wonders and manifestations, the wonders of one god being otherwise than the wonders of another and manifested in their several different manners. There be the wonders and manifestations of Jupiter, of whom I durst not speak in the presence of his undoubted son, there be again the wonders and manifestations of Venus [*cheers from all present and from* ALEXANDER] and these on the other hand be of the wonders of Bacchus, that a man beholding one thing thinketh it two. And the cause and reason of it is this, that Bacchus increaseth as it were the joy and pleasure of all things, giving to the humble man a crown, and to the king two crowns. And in the like manner it is so with the sight of the eyes, that when there is but one thing to the uninspired yet it becometh two to the adorer of Bacchus, and so also again in like manner . . .

ALEXANDER

Crown him with roses. [*With great acclamation he is crowned with roses and led away, men bowing and strewing roses before him.*] We have spoken much of folly and of wisdom—indeed they are one and the same—but we have spoken naught of the glory of Alexander. I will outriot Bacchus. Bring me the jewelled cups of Indian kings, I will have no silver goblets. [*He casts one down.*] Bring me the heavy, huge, Carmanian orchids. Bring women with their diverse Asian silks and dark, dark hair so full of subtle perfumes, and let them be the daughters of old kings, stars that have paled before me at my rising, what time I dawned on Asia. [*He rises from his throne and stands at his full height and all the crowd abase themselves in Oriental fashion.*] I bid you riot, riot, I say riot.

[*Enter* NEARCHOS. *He strides firmly in and walks right up to* ALEXANDER. *He bows respectfully but not in the Eastern manner.*]

NEARCHOS

Is this Alexander?

ALEXANDER

Even Alexander.

NEARCHOS

Is this the state that should be kept by the world's conqueror?

ALEXANDER

Who can say that but I? Who else has conquered the world? Come, come, Nearchos, drink with us.

NEARCHOS

It is not fitting.

ALEXANDER

True, for you are ten goblets behind the soberest of us—but we will none of us start until you have drunk ten goblets.

SCENE I   *ALEXANDER*

NEARCHOS
It is not fitting, for it is a time to mourn.

ALEXANDER
Why, O Nearchos?

NEARCHOS
Because I have seen trembling and shaking to and fro the hand that holds the holy sceptre of Asia.

ALEXANDER
Why? Does it shake? No one has told me this.

NEARCHOS
Hold forth thy sword, Alexander.

[ALEXANDER *holds it out; it shakes.*]

NEARCHOS
See.

ALEXANDER
There is a wind that blows across the plains that shakes my sword. My hand is not shaking.

NEARCHOS
There were great winds at Issus. There thy sword shook not.

ONE
Bah, old man, bah.

ALEXANDER ACT III

ANOTHER

The night's cold and the sheep are coughing. Go and talk to the sheep.

ALEXANDER

My hand shakes.

A THIRD [*with drunken solemnity*]

What you say about Alexander's sword, what you say about his sword, is a lie, what you say about his sword.

ALEXANDER

Trouble him not! It is true! My hand shakes.

NEARCHOS

Even so.

ALEXANDER

My hand shakes. Hither, Nearchos. What do men say of me?

NEARCHOS

They say that Alexander is not to be found in the great cities nor in the council-chambers of kings, but in some wayside place drinks or sings foolish songs and remembers not who he was or what he has done.

ALEXANDER

And what say you?

SCENE I   *ALEXANDER*

NEARCHOS

I say that [*pointing at* ALEXANDER] this is not Alexander, of whom they say these things; for Alexander was wise and temperate, a valiant, austere soldier. I say this is not Alexander.

ONE

Old man, your head will be put into a bucket of muddy water and held there a long time.

ALEXANDER [*almost embracing* NEARCHOS]

Tell me, Nearchos, old friend, what should I do?

SOME

Go away old man, go forth and cough among the sheep.

ALEXANDER

Do not heed these. What should I do, Nearchos?

NEARCHOS

Come as of old to Greece. Be seen in Athens. Rule men as of old from some great city, Persepolis or Athens.

ALEXANDER

No. But from Babylon. I'll blaze upon the world from Babylon. There I'll put on the holy crown of Asia.

ALEXANDER

NEARCHOS [*admiring*]

Babylon?

ALEXANDER

Even from that great city. I'll be your leader once again, Nearchos.

NEARCHOS

Aye. Babylon.

ALEXANDER

Thence we will conquer the Amazons and their queen. Nearchos, I am Alexander yet.

[NEARCHOS *kneels and takes* ALEXANDER'S *hand, abasing his head below it.*]

Curtain

ACT III

Scene II

The Hall of the Fates. Dresses and all are grey.

Curtain rises. ATROPOS *rises and snips a thread, drops shears on floor near* LACHESIS *and goes back to her seat.*

LACHESIS
Ah Destiny, Destiny.

CLOTHO
How long, how long we have laboured, three grim grey women at the woof

LACHESIS
In the time of Zeus the father and the old time of Chronos before him.

CLOTHO
How many threads I have spun.

LACHESIS
How many threads I have woven. Always she cuts our threads, not even one has escaped her.

CLOTHO

Our poor grey threads were but of tears and laughter, of tears and laughter I spun them, O my sister, but now I have given thee a thread of gold.

LACHESIS

It is indeed of gold, how bright it is and what a joy for our eyes. Is this that dances along it that holy thing named light?

CLOTHO

It is even light, my sister.

LACHESIS

Is it not wonderful? I would that Destiny had permitted God to place our lot amongst the fields of men.

CLOTHO

It is no lot to be desired, my sister; for men are shadows in Hades, as thou knowest, save only a very few.

LACHESIS

Yet to have seen the sun!

CLOTHO

He whose thread we weave and spin shall surely look long on the sunlight.

LACHESIS

Shall not our terrible sister be able to shear it asunder?

SCENE II *ALEXANDER*

CLOTHO
She shall not close her shears on so glad a thread, for is it not the joy of our dark house?

LACHESIS
Yet hath she sundered all, our most swift sister.

CLOTHO
Her shears have only clipped the thin grey threads, the little thin grey threads of tears and laughter; they will not close upon our golden thread. What a thread I have spun thee, even I, Clotho.

LACHESIS
It is indeed of gold, and a great thread and a strong one.

CLOTHO
Never before have we seen a thread of gold and a thread not for Atropos. Never before danced light on the grey woof of thy weaving.

LACHESIS
Whose life is it I weave with the golden cord not for Atropos?

CLOTHO
I have spun for thee Alexander.

LACHESIS

Alexander, Alexander. Surely kings were his forbears that he brings the shimmer of light to our grey house and to our weaving.

CLOTHO

My earth dreams that came down from the fields where light is and greenness tell how a queen was his mother, and how some say that his father was King of Macedon, and others that he was Zeus, the child of Chronos.

LACHESIS

Never was such a thread. Alexander, O Alexander.

CLOTHO

The best thread of my spinning.

LACHESIS

He shall have our love for the light that he brought to our dark house, and our aid in the fields of greenness.

CLOTHO

We will give him strength in the world, in the fields that look on Apollo.

LACHESIS

We will give him the throne of a king, and many crowns for his footstool.

SCENE II *ALEXANDER*

CLOTHO

We will give him victory, and kingdoms by right and by conquest.

LACHESIS

Are we not the Fates to reward a man as it please us?

CLOTHO

What more should a man desire of the gods, or of dark Destiny that sits behind them, than the friendship and the favour of us, three ageless women sitting at the woof?

LACHESIS

She doth not speak, our sister Atropos.

CLOTHO

What should she say though she spoke? It is a sweet thing to spin, and to weave is sweet; and pleasant it is to speak of the thin grey threads that I spin of tears and laughter, to be glad for a little while and to see the sun. But of what should she speak, and what words can she say, save only, "I have ended, I have ended"?

LACHESIS

Indeed she seldom speaks, and what should she say? For surely Destiny has given her no pleasant task to tell of, but a sad task to do swiftly.

ALEXANDER ACT III

ATROPOS
Give me the shears.

LACHESIS
Oh, Atropos.

Curtain

ACT IV

Scene I

Babylon, just inside the great gateway, under the towers. In the centre a black pyramid of steps with a golden throne on top of them.

1st Archer

We've been here a weary time.

2nd Archer

Yes, comrade, but we shall see Alexander crowned in Babylon.

1st Archer

Yes, surely.

2nd Archer

A sight such as the ages have not seen.

1st Archer

Will it be very glorious?

2nd Archer

It is scarcely to be thought of. The great captains will come first with their guards, and the ambassadors of the three great nations with their barbarians. These will be here to welcome him. Then he comes and we all make obeisance, Greeks and barbarians together. And he will go up and sit upon the throne and put the crown of Asia on his head.

1ST ARCHER

And then, comrade?

2ND ARCHER

Then we shall all cry out and worship him.

1ST ARCHER

And after he has put the crown upon his head and we have worshipped him?

2ND ARCHER

Why then the princes come up on elephants, and the camel men will go by with the golden trumpets. Men say that it will be the grandest scene in the history of the world, either past or future.

1ST ARCHER

Either past or future?

2ND ARCHER

So the historians say, and the prophets also.

1ST ARCHER

And we shall see it.

SCENE I   *ALEXANDER*

2ND ARCHER

Yes, we shall see it.

1ST ARCHER

And when shall we fight again?

2ND ARCHER

They say that when he is crowned Alexander will move with his whole army and the three great nations against the neighbouring Amazons, and bring Queen Rhododactilos to this place and wed her with great ceremony.

1ST ARCHER

Ah, then there will be more pomp. Alexander did not always love great shows.

2ND ARCHER

No, not always, but things are different now. Do you remember Hipporax of the Hoplites?

1ST ARCHER

Yes. A blunt, honest fellow, but careless with his tongue.

2ND ARCHER

He is condemned to death.

1ST ARCHER

What for?

ALEXANDER

2ND ARCHER

Blasphemy.

1ST ARCHER

What did he say?

2ND ARCHER

He said that Alexander has a fever.

1ST ARCHER

Well, it is marshy land round Babylon, many have fever, why not . . . ?

2ND ARCHER

Hush. How can fever touch the sons of God?

1ST ARCHER

Is Alexander truly the son of Zeus?

2ND ARCHER

He has said so, and the priests do not deny it: that is enough for us.

1ST ARCHER

It will be enough for poor Hipporax. Well, well, his tongue was too long and it was bound to hang him. When will he die?

2ND ARCHER

After the proclamation of Alexander as son of God and emperor of Asia.

SCENE I *ALEXANDER*

1ST ARCHER

Poor Hipporax. It is hard that one man should be the son of God while another should be a poor soldier.

2ND ARCHER

Do not speak treason.

1ST ARCHER

I do not speak treason, I only . . .

2ND ARCHER

Hush, the great captains come.

[*Enter* GREAT CAPTAINS, AMBASSADORS, *retinue.*]

PTOLEMY [*to the three* AMBASSADORS]

And when he places the crown upon his head you will all cry out, rendering homage to him in the name of your people and of your god. And when this is done *you* will cry out and render homage in the name of *your* people and of your god also. After which *you* will cry out in like manner and render homage unto him in the name of *your* people and god.

A GREEK

And what shall *we* do when he places the crown upon his head?

PTOLEMY

You will also render homage in the name of your god.

GREEK

Our god is Zeus.

PTOLEMY

Ah, yes. You kneel upon the lowest step and ask whether he be content to receive homage on behalf of Olympian Zeus. He will doubtless say that it were not meet that the father should pay homage to the son. You will then retire, making obeisance, and the elephants come up. Where is the commander of the elephants?

COMMANDER OF ELEPHANTS

Here, Ptolemy.

PTOLEMY

Is all ready?

COMMANDER OF ELEPHANTS

It is ready.

PTOLEMY

That is well.

COMMANDER OF ELEPHANTS

Upon what signal do the elephants march?

PTOLEMY

When we all hail him as the son of God. Where is the captain of the camel-guard?

CAPTAIN OF CAMEL-GUARD

Here, Ptolemy.

SCENE I   *ALEXANDER*

PTOLEMY

When the elephants kneel by the throne the camel-guard goes by behind them at the walk, the musicians playing.

CAPTAIN OF CAMEL-GUARD

Yes, Ptolemy.

PTOLEMY

What music have you commanded them to play?

CAPTAIN OF CAMEL-GUARD

The song that Marthos made in honour of God.

PTOLEMY

Ah, very good. On the golden trumpets?

CAPTAIN OF CAMEL-GUARD

Yes, Ptolemy.

PTOLEMY

That is well. And then? What follows then?

PARÁXONĒS

Then I come when the camels have gone past.

PTOLEMY

Who are you?

ALEXANDER   ACT IV

PARÁXONĒS

I lead the dance of the thousand women.

PTOLEMY

Ah yes, when the camels have gone past, yes. And then the priests of all the gods in the world. You all know your stations. [*A murmur.*] That is well. Now when the procession arrives you kneel upon the ground but do not prostrate yourselves till he crowns himself.

> [*A woman comes on coughing. A sentry puts out his arm barring the way without looking at her.*]

SHE

Let me come, let me come. I'll see Alexander crowned.

SENTRY

You cannot come here, mother, this place to-day is sacred.

PARÁXONĒS

What! Did I not hear Thais? [*He looks straight at her and then round about.*] Did I not hear Thais?

THAIS

Yes, it is Thais. Thais with a cough, and not immortal like Alexander.

SCENE I   *ALEXANDER*
                    PARÁXONĒS
Thais!
[*Enter an* ARCHER.]

                    ARCHER
The procession is coming.

                    PTOLEMY
To your places.

            AMBASSADOR OF THE ARABS
Must we kneel now?

                    PTOLEMY
No. Not till he comes to the cypress. All kneel then. [*To the* ARCHER.] Where is he?

                    ARCHER
He is past the palm-trees.

                    PTOLEMY
Be ready. I shall give word and all kneel together. [*To the* ARCHER.] Has he come to the cypress?

                    ARCHER
The procession has stopped.

                    PTOLEMY
Stopped? For what cause?

ARCHER

I cannot see the cause. Alexander stops. . . .
Now he comes on again.

PTOLEMY

Now is he by the cypress?

ARCHER

He has stopped again.

PTOLEMY

He has stopped, you say?

ARCHER

Yes, he has stopped to speak to a veteran soldier. . . . He is on again now.

PTOLEMY

Has he come to the cypress?

ARCHER

He is just nigh it.

PTOLEMY [*raising his hand*]

Let all men kneel.

ARCHER

Now he has stopped again. He speaks to one of his escort. Now he comes on.

SCENE I *ALEXANDER*

PTOLEMY
Where is he now?

ARCHER
He is not much past the cypress. The procession moves slowly. And now he stops to speak to another soldier.

PTOLEMY
Rise up till I give the word again.
[PTOLEMY *goes to the high place.*]

ARCHER
Now he comes on once more. Ah, but he stops to speak again. He sits down as he speaks. He is seated upon a log.

PTOLEMY [*on the high place*]
Hither, Perdiccas!
[PTOLEMY *and* PERDICCAS *exchange glances on the high place by the* ARCHER.]
Now he is coming. You may kneel again.
[*Enter* ALEXANDER.]

ALEXANDER
Did I not say, "I will come to Babylon"?

PTOLEMY
Indeed, you said it, Alexander.

Alexander

I *have* come to Babylon. [*Pause.*] I am with friends; I have no need of armour. [*He removes his helmet. The procession advances.*] Halt. Hither, Ptolemy. I would show my trust in Ptolemy; march at my right hand. [*He puts his arm round his neck.*] And you also, Perdiccas— my trust in you—I would show that also—march at my left [*he puts his other arm round* Perdiccas's *neck*], but slowly, for many of our men are weary, slowly Perdiccas. [*He comes on thus supported.*]

Ptolemy

I fear your Grace is ill.

Alexander

Ill, Ptolemy? Ill? No, no. Fatigued perhaps a little. A man may be fatigued who has conquered the world. I am not ill.

Perdiccas

I fear your Grace is ill.

Alexander

I say I am not ill. What illness should there come to the sons of God. I am tired, Ptolemy, a little tired.

Ptolemy

We will assist your Grace.
   [*They come to the steps.*]

SCENE I   *ALEXANDER*

ALEXANDER

Stop, Ptolemy. No mortal man shall tread these steps of onyx. I must go up alone. [*He ascends. He stops, panting.*] It is a fitting throne for the son of God. [*He goes on. He sits down.*] I am tired, Ptolemy. [*He tries to crawl higher, he falls prone on a step.*] I have conquered the world and I am tired.

AMBASSADOR

Your son of Zeus is sick.

ALEXANDER

Sick! I say that sickness comes not to the immortals. I say that I am immortal like my father, whom Chronos begat in the old time.

[1ST AMBASSADOR *moves away contemptuously with his men. Men come up the steps and lift up Alexander.*]

Up. Up to the throne. I say up.

[*They carry him down. The* ARABS *and* NOMADS *crowd up, and look curiously.*]

Kneel, Arabs and you, people of the Nomads, kneel; for I am the immortal son of Zeus.

[*They do not kneel.*]

Ptolemy! Ptolemy! What is this, Ptolemy! They dare to disobey Alexander.

PTOLEMY

They do not understand. They are an untutored people.

ALEXANDER

ALEXANDER

They understand me when my sword is out. Then they are tutored. Give me my sword.

[*They lay him upon a litter.*]

Give me my sword.

[*One draws it and puts it into his hand. It falls to the ground.*]

Give me my sword.

ONE [*to* ANOTHER]

No, no, it is too heavy.

ALEXANDER

Kings have found it so. [*Clutching at his heart.*] But what is this? I am the heir of Philip. I inherit! I inherit from Philip of Macedon what he had from his father, the same that his father had from the old time.

SYCOPHANTES

Indeed you inherit Macedon. Yet are you the son of Zeus though heir to Philip.

ALEXANDER

It is not Macedon that I inherit now, but man's sure legacy, the human heirloom—even death. O Philip, my father, by this I know that I am your son and heir. Philip of Macedon, my father, my father.

ONE

He does not say he is the son of Zeus.

SCENE I *ALEXANDER*

ALEXANDER

Philip my father, for how long have I disowned you. What has man to do with his betters that he should claim kinship with the immortal gods?

[*Enter* PRIEST.]

PRIEST

Is it not time to repent and to turn to the most high gods, and will you not make peace with Apollo now?

ALEXANDER [*to a* HERALD]

Go you to Delphi and to the sacred shrine, and kneel in the doorway and call the name of Apollo, and having called it thrice repeat these words: "Thus saith Alexander: Behold I am going down into the dark and the long way that man knows not. Yet think not that the victory is with Apollo, for with my scant hours I have left a name that his long long days shall not surpass in glory." Say that I envy not to the gods their calm, untroubled faces——

PRIEST

Oh, Blasphemy!

ALEXANDER

Aye, for it is easy for them to have ageless calm who are not vexed by time or the ills of Earth.

Priest

Be guided even yet by the gods in this your last hour.

Alexander [*to the* Priest]

Hath a god died that they should presume to show the way to a traveller bound for a country to which they durst not go? Rather teach your god how to die, saying: Thus died Alexander. [*To the* Herald.] And tell Apollo that it is well for the gods I die; for had I wedded Rhododactilos, that fair and terrible queen, we had reared up such a progeny as had overthrown the gods and taken from them Olympus by force of arms.

[*He dies.*]
[*They all desert the body of* Alexander. *Either night comes on and passes, or the curtain falls for a moment representing the passage of night.*]

Curtain

ACT IV

Scene II

*The same. All empty, just before dawn.
The body of* Alexander *lies neglected, covered by a white sheet. It lies in the same part of the stage, in the same position, and at the same angle as did the statue of Xerxes in Act I, and prophecy is fulfilled.*

The curtain rises. Perdiccas *slips in. He goes to the great steps furtively. He climbs them. He picks up* Alexander's *crown that lies upon a step. He sits on the throne. He crowns himself.*

Perdiccas

Ah-h-h-h.
　　[*Enter* Ptolemy.]

Ptolemy

Over what do you crown yourself?

Perdiccas

Over Macedon and the whole of Hellas.
　　[Ptolemy *marches up the steps till he comes to the cloak. He dons it, looking at* Perdiccas.]

Ptolemy

With this cloak I cloak myself. It is of Grecian work. Grecian hands made it. That is the crown of Asia. Egyptians wrought it; you are barbarously crowned over barbarous kingdoms. For me, Macedon.

PERDICCAS

By my crown I will not rule over barbarians.

PTOLEMY

By my sword I will have Macedon.

PERDICCAS

And I, Ptolemy? Have I no sword?

PTOLEMY

I know not. I do not see it.

PERDICCAS [*drawing and holding the sword forward in* PTOLEMY'S *face*]

See it, Ptolemy.

[PTOLEMY *draws; he moves about seeking to come at* PERDICCAS.]

PTOLEMY

You are on a high place, Perdiccas.

PERDICCAS

A high place, Ptolemy.

PTOLEMY

If we were level this matter were soon settled.

SCENE II *ALEXANDER*

PERDICCAS

I am on a high place. This is the throne of Macedon.

[PTOLEMY *goes round behind.* PERDICCAS *turns too.*]

Take Asia, Ptolemy.

PTOLEMY [*with scorn*]

Asia!

PERDICCAS

Then Egypt!

PTOLEMY

Egypt!

PERDICCAS

The kingdoms of Egypt, the Upper and the Lower.

PTOLEMY

A land of dogs!

PERDICCAS

See, I will give to you their barbarous crown. You shall be King of Egypt.

PTOLEMY

Am I not Ptolemy? What should I have to do with Egypt?

PERDICCAS
Here I stand King of Macedon.

PTOLEMY
I will be King of Macedon and all Hellas.

PERDICCAS
No, I am King, and crowned. You shall be King of Egypt.
> [*Enter* NEARCHOS. *He looks upon the corpse of* ALEXANDER.]

NEARCHOS
So he is dead and there are no more kings.
> [PERDICCAS *looks at* NEARCHOS *uneasily. He transfers his sword to his left hand.*]

PERDICCAS
Your hand, Ptolemy.
> [PTOLEMY *also looks at* NEARCHOS *uneasily, clasps hands with* PERDICCAS. *They put up their swords. They put off robe and crown.*]

PTOLEMY
Of course he's dead. The old fool. We must offer him Persia.

PERDICCAS
If that old man speaks to the army—they may misunderstand us.
> [NEARCHOS *still gazes mournfully at* ALEXANDER.]

SCENE II   *ALEXANDER*

PTOLEMY
You and I together, with our men, would overcome his following.

PERDICCAS
And after the battle, Ptolemy? There are many wolves in Persia.

PTOLEMY
The Persians do not know how many we lost in India.

PERDICCAS
We must not fight in Persia.

[NEARCHOS *walks slowly towards them.*]

NEARCHOS
Greeting.

PTOLEMY and PERDICCAS
Greeting, Nearchos.

[NEARCHOS *comes on in silence.*]

PERDICCAS
Greeting, King of Persia.

NEARCHOS
So we are kings.

PTOLEMY
Why yes, Nearchos.

NEARCHOS
And I, the old sea-wanderer, King of Persia?

PERDICCAS
Yes, yes, Nearchos.

NEARCHOS
And Alexander unburied?

PERDICCAS
Why, we have had great affairs to attend to.

NEARCHOS
And you are kings also?

PERDICCAS
Why yes, Ptolemy, and I. . . . Is it not so, Ptolemy?

PTOLEMY
Why yes, there must be kings.
    [NEARCHOS *kneels down and bows his head.*]

NEARCHOS
I make obeisance to such kings.

PERDICCAS
But you also, Nearchos—you also shall be a king.

NEARCHOS
Even so, O King; but not of your kind.

SCENE II   *ALEXANDER*

PERDICCAS

Of what kind, O Nearchos,

NEARCHOS

To the old, old troubled kingdom that has known me long, where the rulers rule or die, I shall go back: where revolution is the state occasion, the daily ceremony. There kings are kings indeed. For I go back to mid-ocean by the long ways of the sea, with a helm for my sceptre; and if I rule the long waves well I live, and if I rule them idly then I die, and my people bury me—as you have never buried King Alexander.

PERDICCAS

We had not time to bury Alexander.

NEARCHOS

You had not time. I go now to my kingdom, therefore let us three kings say farewell for ever. I go, but I shall never see the shore, never see promontories of distant land, but I shall reverently hail the earth as the grave of Alexander, by whatever chance this honour come to it, whether his bones rot down to it one by one, or whether you find time to bury him.

PERDICCAS

We offered you kingdoms, Nearchos, and you taunt us, and speak about the sea.

NEARCHOS

If I have need of easy idle kingdoms, why, I shall take them. The sides of Æthiopia are naked near me, and India with her jewels, and the rivers of Persia; Hellas shall hear me singing as I go by at night. I shall take kingdoms if I have the mood; when I grow too old perhaps for the great blue kingdom that yesterday was grey and is white to-morrow; I shall take kingdoms. Do not be easy on your golden thrones.

[*He bows deeply. Exit, perhaps patting* ALEXANDER'S *hand as he goes.*]

We shall not forget you.

PTOLEMY

Let us kill him.

PERDICCAS

We must not fight in Persia.

PTOLEMY

Will he attack us?

PERDICCAS

He has not men enough. He cannot attack us.

PTOLEMY

Crazy old man! He remembers Alexander.

PERDICCAS

His simple mind thinks of the past only.

PTOLEMY

We have the present to see to. Let us talk.

SCENE II   *ALEXANDER*

PERDICCAS

Not here. Let us draw aside privily. Ho, Sentry!
[*Enter* SENTRY.]

PERDICCAS [*moving towards curtains*]
Guard this place. Come not too near it.
[*Exeunt* PERDICCAS *and* PTOLEMY *through double curtains. Enter two* ARCHERS.]

1ST ARCHER

Where are the great captains?

SENTRY

They are in there. None may enter.

1ST ARCHER

We have an urgent matter to report to the great captains.

SENTRY

None may enter.

2ND ARCHER

We were watching in the tower; a man from the high places may report at all times.

SENTRY

None may enter.

2ND ARCHER

We must report.

ALEXANDER ACT IV

SENTRY

They will be out soon. What is it?

ARCHER

What are they doing?

SENTRY

They are dividing the world. They will be out soon.

ARCHER

It's an army.

SENTRY

An army here?

ARCHER

An army coming against Babylon.

SENTRY

Is it a large army?

ARCHER

It will seem large to us when we are in amongst it.

SENTRY

Fighting then?

ARCHER

It might be.

SCENE II   *ALEXANDER*

Sentry
Who are they?

Archer
I know not.

Sentry
What are they like?

Archer
They carry a palanquin of gold; a thing, I should say, for some god.

2nd Archer
It is not a palanquin, it is a catafalque.

1st Archer
I think it is a palanquin. But you must acquaint the great captains.

Sentry
As it is an army I will acquaint them.
[*Exit* Sentry.]

1st Archer
It is a hard thing, comrade, that none will bury Alexander.

2nd Archer
What matters it what becomes of Alexander now that we are governed by plain honest men?

ALEXANDER

1st Archer

Indeed you are right, comrade. And yet he was worthy perhaps of burial.

2nd Archer

Much has come out of late concerning Alexander.

1st Archer

Why yes. Hath it not? They say, do they not, that he was harsh to our good leaders?

2nd Archer

Indeed, I have it from Perdiccas himself that this was so. Let us be thankful that we are done with him and have plain honest leaders. With Alexander no one knew where he would be a week hence, or what he would say, or what strange plan would come into his head.

1st Archer

Yet some say—do they not—that he was a good soldier?

2nd Archer

There has been much said lately about that.

1st Archer

Not such a soldier, I do not mean, as our captains; yet in his way perhaps a fair man-at-arms.

SCENE II   *ALEXANDER*

2ND ARCHER

I do not think so. At the battle of Issus they say that the orders he gave were ludicrous and had no bearing on the art of war. The captains won the battle.

1ST ARCHER

Is that so?

2ND ARCHER

You have my word for it.

1ST ARCHER

I do not doubt you.

2ND ARCHER

And there is more than this being said of Alexander.

1ST ARCHER

Yet would I have given him burial.

2ND ARCHER

It is better to let him lie, as a warning to all such headstrong people who interfere with plain men that know their own business.

1ST ARCHER

Perhaps it is better.
   [*Enter* PERDICCAS *and* PTOLEMY *arm in arm,* PERDICCAS *wearing the crown.*]

PERDICCAS

And so, Ptolemy, we will settle this matter. [PTOLEMY *shrugs his shoulders*.] It is a fair country. And some day you will come to love the Egyptians almost as though they were—as though they were Greeks.

PTOLEMY

Greeks! But let us hear these men's report.

PERDICCAS

Ah yes. You have come down from a high place?

2ND ARCHER

Yes, your majesty.

PERDICCAS [*pleased and purring*]

Ah-h.

PTOLEMY

Make your report.

2ND ARCHER

A great army is coming against Babylon.

PTOLEMY

A great army?

1ST ARCHER

Yes, it is a great army.

SCENE II   *ALEXANDER*

PTOLEMY
Foot or horse?

2ND ARCHER
Foot. Its vans are already about our walls.

1ST ARCHER
They had marched by night. It was not till dawn we saw them.

PERDICCAS
Ptolemy, Ptolemy. We have let this come upon us, you and I.

PTOLEMY
Well; we will fight them. Is the guard turned out?

2ND ARCHER
The guard is out.

PTOLEMY
And the alarm sounded?

2ND ARCHER
The men are at their posts.

PTOLEMY
We will fight them, Perdiccas.

PERDICCAS
We have not the men.

PTOLEMY

They do not know how many we lost in India.

PERDICCAS

They will find out that if we attack them.

PTOLEMY

Then what's to do?
[*The silver trumpets are heard.*]

PERDICCAS

We must parley.

PTOLEMY

And if they will not parley?

PERDICCAS

Offer them gifts.

PTOLEMY

What shall we offer them?

PERDICCAS

The best we have. Even to India. But we cannot fight.

PTOLEMY

I will not give up Babylon.

PERDICCAS

Even Babylon if they ask it.

SCENE II   *ALEXANDER*

PTOLEMY

But Babylon is the capital of the world. He meant to rule here.

PERDICCAS

Have they good armour?

2ND ARCHER

They are all in mail. They have brazen greaves upon them. Dawn came and we saw them shining.

1ST ARCHER

They were quite close.

PERDICCAS

And they march soldierly?

2ND ARCHER

They come with a fierce stride. They have skirts to their knees like the Greeks and they all swing together.

1ST ARCHER

The greaves beneath were flashing in the light. They march like Macedonians.

PERDICCAS

They could take Babylon, Ptolemy.

PTOLEMY

Ah for the bones that lie in India.

Perdiccas
If we fight, they know our weakness.

Ptolemy
Well, we will parley.

Perdiccas
At the worst we will offer them Asia.

[*Enter* The Queen of the Amazons *with a regiment of guards.*]

Ptolemy
For what purpose have you come up against great Babylon?

Perdiccas
O puissant Queen, we be the conquerors of the world, and yet, within reason, demand of us what you will and go your way in peace, for we be aweary of war. Take India, only go hence.

Queen of the Amazons
I will not go hence.

Perdiccas
Consider India! There are towers there that are all mother-of-pearl; towers of tortoise-shell, and towers of ivory: the archers on them are all armed in silver. There is a city of India walled with onyx, and an old dungeon there in which kings only suffer; the chains on its walls are golden,

SCENE II   *ALEXANDER*

and golden are the fetters in the floor. They say the mire in it is full of crowns.

So famed for turquoises are the Indian hills that it is told me that their peaks in heaven may scarcely be distinguished from the sky, so azure are they with their wondrous jewel.

QUEEN OF THE AMAZONS

I will not be content with India.

PERDICCAS

Consider, O Queen. Its shores are so strewn with pearls where they run down all golden to the sea (whether by divers flinging them on the beach, or by the listless wash of Indian tides) that handfuls may be gathered by all who list.

And more than this was told me in India: for all these things men have told me, but with my own eyes I have seen the elephant, doing his work in battle.

QUEEN OF THE AMAZONS

It is told me how you have within this city, and are all unworthy of it, one of the wonders of the world. Give it up or I burn Babylon.

PERDICCAS

Indeed, O Queen, we have the hanging garden, the same Darius made. It is in ill repair, and it were hard indeed to fetch it hence, yet. . . .

QUEEN OF THE AMAZONS

Give up to me the body of Alexander.

PERDICCAS
Of Alexander? Where is it?

ONE
It lies there.

QUEEN OF THE AMAZONS [*turning*]
Oh Alexander.

PERDICCAS
I hear that you have brought amongst your army, as some men say, a catafalque of gold, and, as others say, the palanquin of some immortal god.

QUEEN OF THE AMAZONS
Indeed I cannot say which of the two it be. He was scarce like to one of the sons of men, but like to the sons of men he is now dead.

[*She goes up to the neglected body.*]

Curtain

THE OLD KING'S TALE

DRAMATIS PERSONÆ

KING HODIATHON.
THARDEES } *Two Lovers.*
ARANIA }
THE HERALD.

THE OLD KING'S TALE

Place: A fair country.
Scene: Anything in the wide world.
Time: Now or never.

KING HODIATHON *is seated upon some steps in the centre back. He is poorly dressed in an old whitish robe. His beard is white.*
Enter two lovers. (She R. He L.)
They meet in the centre of the stage.

THARDEES
What tidings, O Arania?

ARANIA
Oh, evil tidings, Thardees.

THARDEES
Alas. I also.

ARANIA
Oh, what say they, Thardees?

THARDEES
They say that it was not the wish of the gods that two so young should marry   They said that the gods willed otherwise, for this had not been

THE OLD KING'S TALE

before. Had the gods willed it, they said, it must have happened often and been wonted; but it is not customary for the young to wed as young as we.

ARANIA

O Thardees, the gods are silly. What said they, Thardees?

THARDEES

They said it must not be.

ARANIA

O Thardees.

THARDEES

And what said they to you, Arania?

ARANIA

They said the same, Thardees. They said I was too young and the gods did not wish it. They took counsel of the priests and the priests went into their temple, and answered that it was not the wish of the gods. What do the gods know about these things, Thardees?

THARDEES

They should not have troubled the gods.

ARANIA

Why do they do so, Thardees, and make us unhappy?

THE OLD KING'S TALE

THARDEES
They forget their youth.

ARANIA
We will not forget, Thardees, will we?

THARDEES
I do not wish ever to live to be old. I think that after thirty all is sadness.

ARANIA
For us it is sad always. We must part, Thardees.

THARDEES
No, no, Arania. No, not yet. They said: No more after to-day. But to-day is ours, still, Arania. To-morrow belongs to the gods and the old men.

ARANIA
Alas, Thardees! Our days were such happy days: there will be no days like those among the days of the gods and the old men.

THARDEES
Alas, Arania, half our day is gone. Where were you all the morning, O Arania? All the morning I sought you. By our old paths I went and did not find you. You were gone from our woods, and all their ways were mournful.

THE OLD KING'S TALE

ARANIA

O Thardees.

THARDEES

We shall walk their ways no more.

ARANIA

I was on the headland, Thardees. I was looking towards the sea. There was so lovely a ship come into the harbour that I looked at it all the morning. It was all white like a mountain, and beautiful pale-blue pennants flew from the masts over the huge white sails.

THARDEES

That was from a far country.

ARANIA

Yes, some far country. O Thardees, I think it is some lovely country that sends so fair a ship. I think that they dance there, far away, and sing; and wed when they love and know no dreadful gods. And then, Thardees, a herald came from the ship, with a lovely silken gonfalon on his trumpet; and he went the way of the hamlets on the hills, blowing his trumpet in the morning. O Thardees, it was beautiful on the hills.

THARDEES

How had you the heart, Arania, to see beauty upon the hills? The beauty of the hills is gone and the joy of the woods with them. And they that have taken them from us, what will they do

THE OLD KING'S TALE

with them? They are old and have forgotten the way of joy. Why do no sorrows overtake other men?

ARANIA

There are none so luckless as we.

THARDEES

Was ever any man so sad as I?

KING HODIATHON

O Lovers, hear my tale.

[*They turn towards him, noticing him for the first time. They move nearer to him, lifting up their hands a little in surprise.* THARDEES *goes towards his left hand,* ARANIA *towards his right.*]

O Lovers, in a far country my father was the king.

ARANIA

Your father was king?

KING HODIATHON

Yes, in a far country.

ARANIA

King's son, tell us your story.

[*They sit on each side of him.*]

KING HODIATHON

My father sent me upon a journey in the charge of one trusted duke, that I might see the countries

THE OLD KING'S TALE

of the world. So we kissed the beard and sceptre of my father, and set forth on a morning, and came in the course of days to the lands of others. I sojourned long in a land that was near the morning towards the birth of the sun. O Lovers, it was one of the lands of song.

ARANIA

Was it very beautiful? Was it lovelier than our hills?

KING HODIATHON

It was scarcely a hundred leagues, they said, from the very morning. It was nearly a part of the dawn. One day a herald came to the court of the king, my cousin, bearing a gonfalon of crape. My father, that austere beloved prince, was dead.

ARANIA

Ah. Was it long ago?

KING HODIATHON

It was in my youth. The king of that land near the sun (he was named the King of the Morning) gave us a retinue and his choicest camels, for the desert lay between him and the lands that knew my father: we took the way of the desert for sake of speed. In fifty days we should have crossed the desert, and then ten days with horses to see the hills of my home; for I was now the king of that country, and speed was urgent that I might fulfil the sacrifice that was my father's due, at the foot of his sepulchre, while yet his ghost could perceive it, and then reign in his

THE OLD KING'S TALE

stead. We travelled through the desert thirty days. We went the way of the sun. All day we travelled, but before nightfall came we pitched our tents by sunlight on the sand. The sand was like the gold that the rivers sift, which the merchants bring in their shallow onyx cups. The air was cold by night under those great stars, but the soft sand was warm until midnight passed. After the thirtieth day as we travelled towards evening the evil wind blew from the going down of the sun. It blew like the whisper of a woman at night. The gold sands danced to the whisper, and all was whisper and darkness. And we knew it for the wind that all men curse. O Lovers, our camels died!

ARANIA

Oh! And you were fond of your camels.

KING HODIATHON

We were fond of life. Our retinue gave up their water to us; for three days they carried it and would not drink. Nothing could move them from their purpose; it was the command of their king. We could not cross the desert now, but we struck southwards to find the desert's edge, where the dark forest is. On the fourth day all our retinue died, and the duke from my country and I went on southwards over the sand.

[*He hangs his head and is silent.*]

ARANIA

And then?

THE OLD KING'S TALE

KING HODIATHON
Then we were alone.

ARANIA
And so you came to the dark forest?

KING HODIATHON
My brave companion died. There was only water for one and he would have it so. He would not drink and he died. I alone came, on the tenth day, to the forest.

ARANIA
You found water there?

KING HODIATHON
There were huge nameless rivers.

THARDEES
Sir, you have told us a sad tale indeed; yet we who love each other lose more than comrade, retinue and camels. There is none so sad as we.

KING HODIATHON
O Lovers, I lived for a year amongst naked men. Meanly I lived amongst a savage people. For all that year I did not see the sun, but only the glint of it on great leaves above me. They hunted with little bows and had no king and worshipped rats as gods.

ARANIA
Was it very dark in the forest?

THE OLD KING'S TALE

KING HODIATHON
It was the home of darkness. I lived there for a year. Sometimes the shadow of it falls on my mind, in these years, even now.

ARANIA
Oh, it was long ago; you must forget it.

KING HODIATHON
At times the shadow of huge trees falls on my mind.

ARANIA
There are no shadows here. It is all sunlight.

KING HODIATHON
At the end of that evil year there was talk in the huts. A party of the savage men were going on a journey. They talked in the evenings and pointed. They seemed to point northwards. One evening they all slipped away, running softly. I joined them and they let me come. There was a way over the desert that they had learned. I crossed the desert with them, going northwards. I left them at night, and never learned why they had made the journey. I walked northwards many days through an unknown land and came to the borders of a country I knew. To west of it lay my home.

ARANIA [*gladly*]
Oh!

THE OLD KING'S TALE

KING HODIATHON

O Lovers, there was war in that country!

ARANIA [*sadly*]

Oh!

KING HODIATHON

No man might cross it. No one knew me there. I tarried long on the border. I toiled, as I had learned to toil, with my hands. A year passed by. Still there was war in that country. I waited still on the border toiling with my hands. Another year was gone. I lived in a rude hut that I built of reeds by the river. The war raged on and the third year went by. O Lovers, I was five years from my home.

I would wait no longer then, but set out north for the mountains, for there was a way round that country by a pass in the Northern Crags. I travelled for a year. I came to the pass far up on the shoulders of those great mountains. The heads of the mountains looked down on me in silence. The Blue Glacier had moved. O Lovers, the pass was blocked.

ARANIA

O Thardees, there are other sorrows than ours.

KING HODIATHON

I travelled back again, and a year went over my wanderings. The war was over in the country I knew. I walked across it a worn, derided wan-

THE OLD KING'S TALE

derer. I walked begging my bread. I came in the passing of days at last near the western boundary. I thought then soon to be home.

O Lovers, their king was dead and no man reigned.

Arania

Did they harm you? Were they at enmity with kings?

King Hodiathon

They were searching for a king. One day when I was nearly free of their country a man stopped and looked at my eyes. O maiden, there is something in the eyes of a king that cannot be concealed. They took me from my road and made me their king.

O Lovers, it was a country of dogs. Their ways were evil. I sought to escape, but they would have a king. They brought me back to their palace. I sent messengers to my country, but they killed them. Again I sought to escape and they brought me back. A third time I tried, O Lovers. That people pursued me and overtook me again. And that third time they stripped me of my robe; of my silken vestments they stripped me and took back their crown, and gave me my rags again and cast me out. O Lovers, it was on the far side they cast me out, across their eastern boundary. To the wrong side of their country they drove me away. I was a beggar again, and my own country was still without a king. They would not let me cross their frontier any more. To the North the huge Blue Glacier

THE OLD KING'S TALE

lay in the pass. I walked to the South and so came back to the Desert. [ARANIA *weeps*.] O maiden, weep not yet. You know not yet the sorrow of my story. At the Desert's edge I came on a caravan so suddenly which was going the way of my country, that I believed my gods were guarding me. They took me with them westwards and no wind blew; it was the fairest season the desert knows. I drew near to my own country.

ARANIA

After so long.

KING HODIATHON

O maiden, there lives a people in the Desert more evil than the wind that all men curse. O maiden, they attacked our caravan. A people with terrible spears. As a slave they sold me far off in a city by the sea.

THARDEES

Oh, woeful tale!

ARANIA [*sorrowfully*]

You had no hope then.

KING HODIATHON

I was not broken yet. Know that in my far country are harbours of the sea.

ARANIA

Were you near your own country?

THE OLD KING'S TALE

KING HODIATHON

I was far and far away. Yet I had hope from the sea.

ARANIA

And did ships put out from that city for your country?

KING HODIATHON

I was a slave. No ship would take me.

THARDEES

How had you hope from the sea?

KING HODIATHON

Lovers, behold that tree. As it lies there, a huge log lay near the water in the city where they enslaved me. It was huge like that and forsaken, and near by the place of our toiling. I hollowed it out with knives. Behold how I hollowed it. [*He goes to the tree.*] I cut below it thus, and carried the cuttings away. I hollowed it out below. I worked in the darkness. My eyes never beheld the work of my knife. I hollowed it a little every day and no man knew of the hollowing. It lay thus always, still a smooth round tree. Then I made masts for it and laid them underneath. I made a sail of rags and secreted it thus.

ARANIA

You must have worked on it for many days.

KING HODIATHON

O Lovers, I carved that boat in seven years!

THE OLD KING'S TALE

Arania

In seven years!

Thardees

O Arania, there are sorrows greater than ours.

King Hodiathon

Not yet. You have not heard yet the sorrow of my story. When the seven years were gone I told the gang—we were twenty slaves in my gang—I told them that there was an order from one of the slave-drivers that the tree was to be pushed further down the beach. They believed me and we all pushed it down, and we left it when the tide was out, at a place between the high and the low.

I did this on an evening. At nightfall I slipped away. I went down to the water where the bloodhounds could not scent me. When they counted the slaves they would have searched the ships, and then they would have searched the booths in the city where the strong wine is for which the slaves risk death; for a slave does not run away to the bare sea. But in a while I heard the bloodhounds coming.

Arania

Oh!

King Hodiathon

O maiden, the tide was in. Before the boat quite floated I turned it over, the water helping me with one edge down on the sand. I was in the boat and casting the water out when I heard

THE OLD KING'S TALE

the bloodhounds coming. Then the tide came in and I pushed off in the darkness.

I set up the mast that night and hoisted my sail. O maiden, the wind was blowing towards my country.

I sailed before that strong wind ten days and eleven nights. Dawn came and I saw the spires of my native land, glittering low in the morning.

ARANIA

O exiled king, you saw your native land.

KING HODIATHON

I saw my native land. A contrary wind arose, rising up with the dawn. And then, O Lovers, O Youth that asks what man is sad as you, O Lovers, then I knew that the gods were against me.

[ARANIA *weeps afresh.* KONG HODIATHON *ceases to speak.*]

THARDEES

Oh, tell us your tale.

KING HODIATHON

There is no more to tell: I knew that the gods were against me.

THARDEES

You never landed on your native coast?

KING HODIATHON

No, I was cast upon far distant shores.

THE OLD KING'S TALE

THARDEES

You never came by land to your own country?

KING HODIATHON

I sought to come no more. In many lands I have wandered. The gods are against me.

ARANIA

Do the gods never relent? [*Temple bells are heard.*] Hark! The bells of our temples. They say in our country that when those sweet bells ring on passing winds at evening that then the gods are at peace with all men within the sound of those bells.

KING HODIATHON

I do not hear them.

ARANIA [*she lays a hand on his*]

Is there no help against the gods?

KING HODIATHON

Yes! Against one thing the gods are weak. They are like a fortress of adamant with one fragile door. Against youth alone they are weak. They durst not crush youth. The gods durst not. Go against them, O Lovers, and prevail.

ARANIA

We do not think of our sorrow any more. Oh, let us comfort you, poor wandering king. Go in our woods. Be happy in the beauty of our hills.

THE OLD KING'S TALE

Are they not perhaps as fair as your own far country nearly?

KING HODIATHON
Ah, yes. Your hills are fair.

ARANIA
They are beautiful, our hills. And all this morning a herald walked along them, come from a beautiful ship, a light-blue banner floated from his trumpet as he went along the hills, and the sun was shining on him all the morning.

KING HODIATHON [*without emotion*]
Light blue? Why, that would be the banner of my country.

ARANIA
Of your country! The ship is there! The great ship in the harbour!

[*He looks downward and is silent. The sound of a trumpet is heard.*]

Hark!

[*Words are heard off, amongst which you distinguish "Hodiathon" and then "a far country."*]

THARDEES
It is the herald!

[KING HODIATHON *remains seated. Enter R. the* HERALD. *A light blue banner of silk hangs from his trumpet. He blows his trumpet and halts.*]

THE OLD KING'S TALE

HERALD

Hath any here tidings of King Hodiathon, the lord of a far country?

[KING HODIATHON *watches him in silence.*
The Lovers watch the King in delighted, breathless expectancy.
The HERALD *marches on. Exit L.*]

ARANIA

But you are the *King!*
[*The trumpet is heard again.*]

HERALD [*off*]

Hath any here tidings of King Hodiathon, the lord of a far country?

KING HODIATHON [*to* ARANIA]

No, no. It would be useless. The gods are against me. . . .
Fight them! Fight the gods! They cannot stand against youth.

[*The Lovers rising,* THARDEES *takes* ARANIA *in his arms.*]

THARDEES

Love, let us fight the gods.

Curtain

THE EVIL KETTLE

THE EVIL KETTLE

Scene: The House of Mrs. Watt.
Time: Tea time.

A room in a cottage. Window in centre of back looking out upon pleasant hills. Cupboard at right of back. Door R. near back. Table in centre. Fireplace left. Couch or sofa along wall L. with head touching back. This is as I see it, but all details are unimportant except the hills, and should not fetter the initiative or fancy of a producer. JAMES WATT, *a lad of fifteen or sixteen, is leaning with folded arms on the window sill, looking at the hills. It is what is called a "costume play," period about 150 years ago.*

MRS. WATT *is laying the tablecloth.*

MRS. WATT

Tea time.

JAMES WATT [*glancing over his shoulder and back again to window*]

Yes, Mother.

[*He goes on looking at the hills.*]

MRS. WATT [*going on smoothing out the tablecloth*]

Come on.

THE EVIL KETTLE

JAMES WATT

How lovely the hills are, Mother.

MRS. WATT

The hills? Of course they are.

JAMES WATT

There's such a golden light on them.

MRS. WATT

Come and watch the kettle.

JAMES WATT

All right, Mother; in a moment. I do so want to look at the hills. They are so lovely.

MRS. WATT

It's past five.

JAMES WATT

And the woods along the top. All the beech came out yesterday. The woods are like brass. Aren't they lovely, Mother?

MRS. WATT

Of course they are. All God's work is lovely. Come and watch the kettle, dearie.

JAMES WATT

What is God's work, Mother?

THE EVIL KETTLE

MRS. WATT

All the things what was intended, of course.

JAMES WATT

Didn't He make everything?

MRS. WATT

Not the ugly things. Satan makes the ugly things.

JAMES WATT

What are the things that were intended, Mother?

MRS. WATT

Oh questions, questions. What a boy it is to ask questions. I wonder if you'll be very wise when you grow up, for all the questions you've asked, or if you'll still be asking questions about everything. Deary me, I wonder.

JAMES WATT

Perhaps I'll be very wise, Mother, and still not know much.

MRS. WATT

I don't see as how that could be.

JAMES WATT

But what are the things that were intended, Mother?

THE EVIL KETTLE

MRS. WATT

Oh, well: woods and hills and flowers and butterflies, and the wind and the rain and the crops, birds and young girls and all that kind of thing. Satan just makes the ugly things. Come on now.

JAMES WATT

But look at the hills, Mother, with that light on them.

[*She goes to the window.*]

MRS. WATT

Yes, there they are. I remember them hills before you were born, or thought of.

JAMES WATT [*meditatively*]

And they're still just the same.

MRS. WATT

Well, I wouldn't say just the same. They seem a little smaller like.

JAMES WATT

But they couldn't be smaller, Mother.

MRS. WATT

Oh, I don't know. The hills are so old they might have shrunk a little.

JAMES WATT

But they couldn't do that, Mother.

THE EVIL KETTLE

MRS. WATT

And they seemed to be brighter, somehow. The summers was warmer when I was young.

JAMES WATT

What would have caused that, Mother?

MRS. WATT

Oh, bless the boy! How can I tell? It was a long time ago and the days just used to be brighter. Come and watch the kettle. Make the tea the moment it boils.

JAMES WATT

Very well, Mother.

[*She prepares teapot. He sits before the fire. She puts bread, plates, etc., on table. The kettle boils.* WATT *stretches out his hand to take it, then he draws it back. He clasps his hands around his knees and sits watching the kettle intently.*]

JAMES WATT

Mother.

MRS. WATT

Well, child, what is it now?

JAMES WATT

There must be great force in a kettle, Mother.

THE EVIL KETTLE

MRS. WATT
In a kettle, child? What ever do you mean?

JAMES WATT
The lid is lifting up and down.

MRS. WATT
Then it's boiling. Make the tea quick.

JAMES WATT
There must be a great force in it, Mother, to lift a lid like that.

MRS. WATT
Bless the child. That's only steam.

JAMES WATT
Mother. I've been thinking that if steam can do that it might move a rod, mightn't it? And the rod might move a wheel.

MRS. WATT
Move a wheel, child?

JAMES WATT
Yes, Mother. And if we could set wheels moving we could do all the work men have to do without ever using horses.

MRS. WATT
Stands to reason you couldn't do it without horses, whatever steam could do.

THE EVIL KETTLE

JAMES WATT

Why, Mother?

MRS. WATT

Why? Always asking why. Well, where does steam mostly come from? It goes up from the horses ploughing when they get hot. So where would you get your steam without them horses? You'd never get enough from them little kettles.

JAMES WATT

But Mother, I'll make big kettles.

MRS. WATT

Go on and make the tea. [*He pours water into the teapot.*] You'll never get a cup of tea to do the work of a horse.

JAMES WATT [*puts teapot on fire while* MRS. WATT *cuts bread, etc.*]

I'll make big kettles when I grow up. [*He gazes at the kettle again.*] Whenever the lids move great iron bars will move with them. I'll fasten the bars to wheels, Mother, and I'll make steam do everything. All the work of the world would be done in the morning, and men could walk about the beautiful hills all the rest of the day.

[*Enter* SATAN R. *He crosses the room and taps* JAMES WATT *on his left shoulder. Stretching out his left arm he beckons to the window and goes there,* JAMES WATT *following, gazing dumbly.*

SATAN *is invisible to* MRS. WATT. *She cannot see him, though looking straight at him.*

THE EVIL KETTLE

At the window SATAN *waves his left hand a few times upwards. Smoke as of factories rises up covering the entire landscape. The noise and clangour are heard of the twentieth century. The smoke lifts and a factory city appears in all its devilish ugliness, with an unsightly yellow poster in the foreground, on which is written:* TAKE MEDICO. THE CURE FOR ALL AILMENTS. SO NICE. *The smoke thickens again and the city is covered. Again it lifts and shows the city: and so on.*

SATAN *points at it. The boy stares speechless.* SATAN *slaps him on the back with cheerful encouragement.* JAMES WATT *turns and stares at* SATAN *with wide eyes and open mouth, motionless in horror at the idea that* SATAN'S *thanks were due to him for this.* SATAN *nods to him.*]

JAMES WATT [*in horror*]

Oh!

[SATAN *passes his hand backwards and forwards before the window as one rubbing out a blackboard. The city and smoke disappear, the hills come back and the noise of the twentieth century ceases.*

When MRS. WATT *hears* JAMES WATT *say* "Oh" *she looks up.*]

MRS. WATT

Why, Jimmy, what ever is the matter?

JAMES WATT

Oh, Mother, he wants me to do a dreadful thing.

THE EVIL KETTLE

MRS. WATT

Why, who wants you, child?

JAMES WATT

But I won't do it, Mother. I won't do it. [*To* SATAN.] I won't—I tell you I won't.

[SATAN *smiles with scornful assurance.*]

MRS. WATT

You won't what, child? You won't what? What ever is it?

JAMES WATT

I won't, I won't.

[JAMES WATT *flies at* SATAN *and beats him with his fists upon his bare black folded arms, not easily reaching higher.* SATAN *goes on smiling with scornful assurance.*]

MRS. WATT

Child, child, what has come over you? What ever are you doing?

[*She goes towards him anxiously.* SATAN *steps back and bows gracefully to* JAMES WATT. *Exit* SATAN.]

JAMES WATT

I won't. I won't.

MRS. WATT

Jimmy, Jimmy, what ever is the matter?

THE EVIL KETTLE

James Watt

He wants me to invent a bad thing. Mother! He wants to spoil our hills. He wants me to do it, Mother. He wants to cover our hills with dreadful things.

Mrs. Watt

Who, child? Who? What ever is come over you?

James Watt

He. He.

Mrs. Watt

Where?

James Watt

He is gone now.

Mrs. Watt

Come to bed, Jimmy. Come and lie down.

James Watt

He shan't spoil our hills.

Mrs. Watt

Come along. Come and lie down now.

James Watt

He shan't spoil our lovely hills.

THE EVIL KETTLE

MRS. WATT

No, no. No one will hurt the hills. That's right, lie down now. I'll look after the hills.

[*She takes his jacket off.*]

JAMES WATT

I won't invent it. I won't.

MRS. WATT

No, you shan't. Now your boots.

[*She takes his boots off.*]

JAMES WATT

I'll never invent it.

MRS. WATT

No, of course you won't, dearie. Now you lie there while I get you something nice. [*He sits up.*] Now lie still, dearie. Lie still. Do as mother says.

JAMES WATT

But, Mother, I want to lock the door for fear he comes again.

MRS. WATT

Lie still, Jimmy.

JAMES WATT

But, Mother, I must lock the door.

THE EVIL KETTLE

Mrs. Watt

I'll lock the door. No one shall come.

[*She locks the door. He lies down. She goes to cupboard. She takes out a bundle of weeds and selects three different varieties, three or four of each. She puts them together in a bunch and wrings the juice out of the stalks into a saucer. She pours the saucer into a cup and fills it with milk.* James Watt *all the while is stirring restlessly. She gives him the cup to drink and pulls the blind down and sits beside his bed.*

There is now no light in the room but the red light of the fire, and it turns the steam from the kettle into a dull red glow.]

James Watt

You locked the door, Mother? You did lock the door?

Mrs. Watt

Yes, dear, the door's locked. Go to sleep. Nobody shall disturb you.

[James Watt *is soothed and lays his head down.*]

James Watt [*quietly*]

They shan't take our hills.

Mrs. Watt

No, no dearie. Go to sleep now.

[*He lies quiet. Re-enter* Satan *through the solid middle of the locked door.*]

THE EVIL KETTLE

JAMES WATT

Mother! Mother! He's come again. He's come again! Don't you see him? He's after our hills, Mother!

MRS. WATT

No one can come, child. I've locked the door. Go to sleep. Go to sleep.

JAMES WATT

He's squatting before the fire, Mother.

[SATAN *has crossed the room and squatted down by the fire in front of the kettle.*]

MRS. WATT

No, no Jimmy. Go to sleep. It's only the steam from the kettle. I'm here; no one shall hurt you.

[JAMES WATT *is silent but stares at* SATAN.]

SATAN

O dear kettle. Evil kettle. Beloved evil kettle. Most dear, most evil kettle. Speak to him again, dear evil kettle.

[*The kettle puffs out steam into* SATAN'S *face; its lid lifts up and down.*]

Yes, speak to him again. He has my work to do. Speak to him. Speak to him. We shall conquer the world, dear kettle, you and I. You

THE EVIL KETTLE

are cold, poor kettle, poor evil kettle. But see; you shall be warm as never before.

> [*He puts his hand into the fire just underneath the kettle. Steam rushes from its spout, the lid shakes.*]

There, poor evil kettle, you are warm now. You are warm now, dear kettle.

> [*He pats the kettle. Steam bursts up from under the devil's hand where he touches it.*]

James Watt

I won't. I won't. I won't invent it. I won't spoil our hills.

Mrs. Watt

Invent what, child? Nothing can spoil our hills. Nothing can spoil them. Invent what?

James Watt

Never mind what, Mother. It shall never be told. I'll never do it, Mother.

Satan

Speak to him once again, beloved evil kettle. [*The kettle puffs out steam.*] Speak to him, evil kettle.

> [*He goes over to the window and raises a corner of the blind and calls up black factory smoke outside with his left hand. He smiles, and waves it away with his right hand with the same motion as before.*]

THE EVIL KETTLE

JAMES WATT

He wants to spoil our hills.

MRS. WATT

Go to sleep now, dearie, go to sleep. There's a good little boy. The herbs will do you a world of good if only you'll go to sleep.

JAMES WATT

But he'll spoil our hills if I don't watch him.

[SATAN *approaches the bed. He stretches out his right hand. He begins to move it before* JAMES WATT's *face as if rubbing out a slate.*]

Mother! He's trying to make me forget! I won't forget! I won't forget! I'll remember. Mother! Help me, Mother. Mother! Never let me go near the kettle, Mother. Don't let me talk of the kettle. It's steam, Mother. Steam and the devil will spoil our hills. O Mother, don't let me, don't let me. Tell me never to invent anything with steam. [*He grips her arm.*] Promise me, Mother! Promise.

MRS. WATT

Yes, yes dear, I promise.

JAMES WATT

Never with steam, Mother. I *won't* forget. They shan't spoil our hills. I . . . O Mother.

MRS. WATT

Yes, dearie.

THE EVIL KETTLE

JAMES WATT

I'm sleepy, Mother.

[SATAN *tiptoes out.* JAMES WATT *sleeps. For a while* MRS. WATT *sits quietly by the bed. Then she looks attentively at the boy's sleeping face and is satisfied.*]

MRS. WATT

Ah, it's those good herbs.

[*She draws up the blind, revealing the cheerful hills, and goes on preparing the table for tea. She makes the tea and puts it on the table. Presently* JAMES WATT *awakes.*]

JAMES WATT

Hullo, Mother. What am I doing here?

MRS. WATT

You was took over queer, Jimmy. Are you all right now?

JAMES WATT

Yes, Mother, I'm all right now. What was the matter with me?

MRS. WATT

Took over queer you was. But I gave you those good herbs what I got from the hills, and they cured you, thank God. That's what He puts them on the hills for, Jimmy, among all the other flowers. They cures folks wonderful.

THE EVIL KETTLE

JAMES WATT

I'm all right now, Mother.

MRS. WATT

Could you fancy a cup of tea?

JAMES WATT

Yes, Mother. Proper, I could.

[*He gets up and comes to the table. The kettle spouts noisily.* JAMES WATT *sits down. The kettle splutters louder.* JAMES WATT *takes up his cup of tea.*]

Thank you, Mother.

[*The kettle makes a still noisier outburst.* WATT *looks round. He rises and goes over to look at the kettle. He sits in the chair before the fire and looks at it. The kettle steams and the lid lifts.* JAMES WATT *gazes at it.*]

MRS. WATT

Come away from that kettle, Jimmy.

JAMES WATT

The kettle can't hurt me, Mother.

MRS. WATT

Come away from the kettle.

JAMES WATT

But I want to watch it, Mother. I want to watch the lid lifting.

THE EVIL KETTLE

MRS. WATT

Jimmy. When you was ill you made me promise you something.

JAMES WATT

Did I, Mother? What was it?

MRS. WATT

Not to let you go near the kettle, Jimmy, nor to let you talk of steam. There didn't seem any sense in it; but there, I gave you my promise.

JAMES WATT

Did I, Mother? But Mother, I've been thinking while I was watching the lid lifting. I've been thinking that, if steam can do that, it might move a rod, mightn't it? And the rod might move a wheel.

MRS. WATT

Move a wheel, child? That's what you said before.

JAMES WATT

Yes, Mother. And if we could set wheels moving we could do all the work men have to do without ever . . .

MRS. WATT

Now come away, Jimmy, and stop thinking that nonsense. You made me promise, you know; and it didn't do you no good last time. You was took queer like. [JAMES WATT *still gazes at the*

THE EVIL KETTLE

kettle.] Go and look at the hills, Jimmy, there's a good boy. There's good in the hills. [*He goes.*] That's right, Jimmy. There's enough good in the hills to keep a body right whatever trouble of mind he had. Go now and look at the hills. When you was quite a little boy, I used to leave you where you could look at them, and I'd go and get on with my work. I knew no harm could come to you from the hills.

[JAMES WATTS *stops half-way, pondering.*]

JAMES WATT

Yes, Mother, they're wonderful; but Mother, I can't have made you promise not to let me talk of steam, I've thought of such a great invention with steam, Mother.

MRS. WATT

You made me promise and I promised you, Jimmy.

JAMES WATT

I can't have known what I was saying.

MRS. WATT

Well, anyway, keep away from the kettle, Jimmy. If I can't stop you talking I promised you that. [*The kettle spouts away.*] I don't like the looks of the kettle neither, now I come to notice. He seems to . . . it seems . . . but that's all nonsense. But, anyway, keep away from it, same as I promised you. Look at the lovely hills, Jimmy.

THE EVIL KETTLE

JAMES WATT

But Mother, I want to think. It's such a wonderful scheme I've thought of, Mother. It's to make steam do all the work that men have to do. The whole day's work, Mother, would be done in an hour, and everyone would be free all the rest of the day.

MRS. WATT

Well, dearie, if you must have steam, get it from the plough horses when they're hot. Good honest beasts. But leave the kettle alone.

JAMES WATT

But Mother, the kind of steam I want must come from kettles.

MRS. WATT [*giving way*]

Oh, well. After all, bless the boy, what harm can he ever do with a cup of tea?

[*She looks at the hills. The sun sets.*
JAMES WATT *sits gazing at the kettle. The hills darken. The fire glows and the kettle appears more evil.*]

Curtain

THE AMUSEMENTS OF KHAN KHARUDA

THE AMUSEMENTS OF KHAN KHARUDA

A room set for expensive supper, in a hotel that is not too particular.
Plenty of champagne.
A discreet WAITER.

1st MAN-ABOUT-TOWN
Kharuda's late.

2nd MAN-ABOUT-TOWN
Some blighters must have been worshipping him.

1st MAN-ABOUT-TOWN
Worshipping Kharuda?

2nd MAN-ABOUT-TOWN
They *do* worship him, you know.

1st MAN-ABOUT-TOWN
Silly blighters.

2nd MAN-ABOUT-TOWN
They do in his own country.

AMUSEMENTS OF KHAN KHARUDA

1st MAN-ABOUT-TOWN

Some sort of a damned god, is he?

2nd MAN-ABOUT-TOWN

Well, *they* think so.

1st MAN-ABOUT-TOWN [*who has become very slightly drunk*]

Well, all I can say is—in that case—we shouldn't have started without him.

2nd MAN-ABOUT-TOWN

Oh, he meant us to all right. Cunning devil, Kharuda. If he wanted to start fair he'd have been here when the flag fell. You'll find he'll still be sober when we're, well, a bit ahead of him.

CISSIE

Here. I won't have Kharuda talked of like that. He's a dear.

1st MAN-ABOUT-TOWN

Here. I say. . . .

CISSIE

What's up?

1st MAN-ABOUT-TOWN

Well, what about me? Aren't *I* a dear?

CISSIE

Yes, Captain, of course you are.

[*Enter the* KHAN KHARUDA.]

AMUSEMENTS OF KHAN KHARUDA

1st Man-about-Town
Ah, here he is.

2nd Man-about-Town
Here you are, old boy.

Kharuda
Ah! Good evening all. Jolly good evening.
[*He kisses* Yvonne *and tries to kiss* Bessie.]
Oh, come on.

Bessie
No, I don't let anyone kiss me that hasn't been introduced. I make it a rule.

Kharuda
I say, Dick——
[*He makes a sign to* 2nd Man-about-Town *with his hand, meaning,* "*Come on: do the trick.*"]

2nd Man-about-Town
His Highness the Khan Kharuda, er—Bessie.
[Kharuda *kisses* Bessie.]

Bessie
It's a rule I always make. You don't mind?
[Kharuda *is now seated facing audience across the table with* Yvonne *on his right and* Bessie *on his left, and next to* Bessie,

AMUSEMENTS OF KHAN KHARUDA

2ND MAN-ABOUT-TOWN *and next to him,* CISSIE, *and then* 1ST MAN-ABOUT-TOWN.]

KHARUDA

I don't mind your rule now that I'm introduced. But you won't make any more rules? What?

BESSIE

No, that's the only rule I make. But I think one ought to stick to one's rules; don't you?

KHARUDA

Oh, yes. Of course.

BESSIE

I had to make it because I was getting so popular. And you know I don't *like* being too popular.

KHARUDA

No, no, of course not.

[YVONNE, *a dark beauty, fixes her eyes on him under languorous lids.* KHARUDA *is drawn towards her.*]

KHARUDA [*in a lower voice*]

You been here long, Yvonne?

[YVONNE *nods.*]

KHARUDA

So sorry.

AMUSEMENTS OF KHAN KHARUDA

1ST MAN-ABOUT-TOWN [*who has been talking with* CISSIE]

I lay ten to *one* he won't win. I lay ten to one.

CISSIE

Don't be silly, Captain.

1ST MAN-ABOUT-TOWN

I lay ten to one.

CISSIE

I say he's got quite a good chance. Quite all right.

1ST MAN-ABOUT-TOWN

I lay ten to one.

KHARUDA

I take you.

1ST MAN-ABOUT-TOWN

That's right, that's right. When I make a drunken bet I do like to find someone sporting enough to . . .

CISSIE

You aren't drunk, duckie. Not what I call really tight, that is. Is he now? Is the Captain drunk?

2ND MAN-ABOUT-TOWN AND KHARUDA

No, no. He's all right.

AMUSEMENTS OF KHAN KHARUDA

1st Man-about-Town

I say I'm drunk: and *I* ought to know. And when I make a drunken bet I say it's very sporting of old joss-god there to take it. That's what I said.

Cissie

Oh, you aren't drunk.

2nd Man-about-Town

No, no, of course not.

1st Man-about-Town

I say I'm drunk. And I ought to know—numbers I've seen—in *all* parts of the world.

Cissie

You're *quite* all right.

Kharuda

What are we betting in?

1st Man-about-Town

Whatever you like, old boy.

Kharuda

No, no; you say.

1st Man-about-Town

Whatever you like.

Kharuda

No, you.

AMUSEMENTS OF KHAN KHARUDA

CISSIE

It makes no difference to joss-god. You'd better say.

1ST MAN-ABOUT-TOWN

Oh well, tenners then.

KHARUDA

And what are we betting *on?*

1ST MAN-ABOUT-TOWN

What *on?*

BESSIE [*to* 2ND MAN-ABOUT-TOWN]

Oh Lord! That's a rummy bet. Doesn't know what horse he's backing.

2ND MAN-ABOUT-TOWN

Oh, it's all one to joss-god. Some poor blighter grubbing at a cotton-crop will have to pay it in tribute if he loses, I suppose. Eh, Kharuda?

KHARUDA

Oh yes. I suppose so.

CISSIE [*to* 1ST MAN-ABOUT-TOWN]

He didn't hear you say Polymeela.

1ST MAN-ABOUT-TOWN

Oh yes, Polymeela. I lay ten to one.

AMUSEMENTS OF KHAN KHARUDA

KHARUDA
Ten to one against Polymeela?

1ST MAN-ABOUT-TOWN
Yes, *he's* no good.

KHARUDA [*drinking*]
Then here's to Polymeela.

1ST MAN-ABOUT-TOWN [*drinking too*]
Polymeela.

CISSIE
Why do you drink to him if he's no good?

1ST MAN-ABOUT-TOWN
'Cause we're *all* no good.
  [KHARUDA *laughs.* CISSIE *cries.*]

CISSIE
Oh Captain. Don't say such things, duckie.

1ST MAN-ABOUT-TOWN
Sorry, Cissie, sorry. I can't help telling the truth sometimes when I'm drunk.

CISSIE
You're not drunk, not what I really call. And you said a *horrid* thing.

AMUSEMENTS OF KHAN KHARUDA

1st Man-about-Town
Well, isn't it true?

Cissie
That's no excuse.

2nd Man-about-Town
Cheer up, Cissie. He didn't mean it. You didn't mean it, did you?

1st Man-about-Town
What does it matter, when I'm drunk? I wouldn't have meant it if I'd been sober. I mean I'd have meant it but I wouldn't have said it. Well, anyway, that's what I mean, but it doesn't sound sense somehow.

Cissie
Oh well: let's cheer up. What about another glass?

[*She fills his and hers, pouring all the way between the two.*]

2nd Man-about-Town
Look out, Cissie. You're spilling it.

1st Man-about-Town [*pointing to table-cloth—then to his head*]
Better there than here.

Cissie
Oh, will you *stop?*

AMUSEMENTS OF KHAN KHARUDA

1st Man-about-Town

Well, isn't it true?

Cissie

I tell you that's no excuse. Can't we have a bit of a drink without you wanting to make us cry?

1st Man-about-Town

Well, it was true.

Cissie

Well, the others don't talk like that. And they're having their drink, aren't they?

1st Man-about-Town [*looking*]

Yes . . . yes. They are. I say, Kharuda, hasn't your religion got some law or other against champagne?

Kharuda

Yes, Charlie, old boy. But then, you see, its laws are *my* laws. I can change *them*, but they can't touch *me*.

[*All laugh except* Kharuda.]

1st Man-about-Town

Pretty bon for you. What?

Kharuda [*enigmatically*]

Perhaps.

AMUSEMENTS OF KHAN KHARUDA

2ND MAN-ABOUT-TOWN
You know, that's the sort of religion that would suit me.

[*Laughter. Amidst the laughter the door opens very, very slowly under a timid hand.*

The WAITER, *who has hitherto hovered silently about the table or stood discreetly out of the way, moves swiftly but still silently to the door. His silence and swiftness save the company from being aware of the intrusion, as he intercepts a native of Asia in the doorway. A palm conceals the native from those at the table.*]

THE NATIVE
Master, I would speak with the Khan Kharuda.

WAITER
He is not here.

NATIVE [*pressing tips of fingers of both hands to his forehead*]
Master, I *know* that he is here.

WAITER
No, no, he is not here. You must go away.

[NATIVE *puts hand inside his robes and fumbles.*]

NATIVE
I saved this in forty years.

[*Hands money.* WAITER *takes it.*]

AMUSEMENTS OF KHAN KHARUDA

WAITER

Wait a minute.

[*He goes to* KHARUDA.]

A gentleman with an urgent message, your Highness; I understood—from the Foreign Office. Shall I show him in?

KHARUDA

Show him in.

2ND MAN-ABOUT-TOWN

I say, Kharuda, that would be just the sort of religion for me.

[*Laughter. The* NATIVE *advances timidly and humbly.* KHARUDA *looks up at him out of the noise of the others' laughter.*]

NATIVE

Sacred Master.

KHARUDA

Well?

NATIVE

My family die.

KHARUDA

You came to me because of that?

NATIVE

Yes, Sacred Master. It is the black sickness.

AMUSEMENTS OF KHAN KHARUDA

KHARUDA [*leans forward, fixing the* NATIVE'S *eyes with his almost terribly*]
Shahmeen Abdullah, they shall live.

NATIVE
All. Sacred Master?

KHARUDA [*catches his breath almost in fear, then*]
All.

NATIVE
Sacred Master, I am poor. I can offer you no sacrifice. . . .

KHARUDA [*waves him away*]
Remember me when you go to Nasilullah, in autumn, ten years hence.

[*The* NATIVE *goes away backwards before the wave of that hand as though compelled by it.*
Among the diners brief wonder has taken the place of laughter. The WAITER *brings back the Occident by closing the door in his best manner.*
Laughter breaks out from all the diners except KHARUDA.]

2ND MAN-ABOUT-TOWN
Kharuda, old boy, you're a wonder.

1ST MAN-ABOUT-TOWN
You shouldn't have bluffed the poor blighter like that. But it was fine bluff.

AMUSEMENTS OF KHAN KHARUDA

CISSIE

Bluff! I never saw any bluff like it.

BESSIE

Best I *ever* saw. Lord! What'd you be like at poker?

[YVONNE, *the dark beauty, is leaning back laughing inaudibly.*]

2ND MAN-ABOUT-TOWN

You old humbug.

KHARUDA [*glancing from face to face*]

My friends. Laugh at all the follies that I share with you. But this—this is different. It is no affair of yours.

2ND MAN-ABOUT-TOWN

The mysterious East, old boy. You can't come the mysterious East over us.

1ST MAN-ABOUT-TOWN

Just as much mystery in one postal district of London as there is in the whole of your East. Just as much. Only in the East there's—more—bluff.

KHARUDA

Leave the East alone, Charlie. You're only concerned with the follies I share with you.

1ST MAN-ABOUT-TOWN [*repeating himself*]

. . . more bluff.

AMUSEMENTS OF KHAN KHARUDA

BESSIE
Lord! If he played poker.

2ND MAN-ABOUT-TOWN
You're an old humbug, Kharuda. Don't be annoyed! I like you the better for it.

KHARUDA [*angrily*]
Speak of the things you know.

1ST MAN-ABOUT-TOWN
Seen a good deal of the world, Dick and I. Should know a good many things.

2ND MAN-ABOUT-TOWN
Well, what do you want us to talk of? What do we know?

KHARUDA
Champagne. Bad hotels. . . .

1ST MAN-ABOUT-TOWN
Damned *good* hotel.

KHARUDA
Horses, a very little. Jockeys. And what you *think* you know—women.

1ST MAN-ABOUT-TOWN
Think we know. I *say*, Cissie.

AMUSEMENTS OF KHAN KHARUDA

Cissie
Oh, he's being funny.

2nd Man-about-Town
I say. *Think* we know. You're an old humbug. And you're trying to bluff *us*.

1st Man-about-Town
I say, Kharuda; no more mysterious East, please.

2nd Man-about-Town
Because it doesn't go down.

[KHARUDA *rises*.]

Bessie
Now don't get angry, old dear.

[*But* YVONNE *is frightened*.]

Kharuda
Do you think, because I share your foolish pleasures, that I am even as you? Am I to be lonely, because I am incarnate? Did I choose you because I deemed you my equals? No, but because between me and men is a gulf so great that, if I cross it, it matters not where! You are only as remote from my spirit as any others.

1st Man-about-Town
Oh, we'll *do* all right. We'll *do*.

AMUSEMENTS OF KHAN KHARUDA

BESSIE [*with sudden spite*]
Aren't we good enough for you, do you mean?

1ST MAN-ABOUT-TOWN
There's not enough mystery in the whole of the East to supply one postal district of London.

[*The* WAITER, *whose job it is to watch, has felt something that frightens him before any of the others except* YVONNE, *who, having the most sympathy with* KHARUDA, *has sensed a danger in him soonest of all.*]

KHARUDA
You shall see.

[*He lifts his arm and opens his hand and brings it down towards the table.*
As the arm descends thunder rolls. This happens three times, darkness coming up rapidly; with the third—black out. Flashes, and a dim light only on KHARUDA'S *head, which is a blue Japanese demon-mask, with ferocious, bristling moustache; yet it is clear that he has not moved, but has merely changed. He points at each one in turn, going left-handed.* BESSIE *first, then* 2ND MAN-ABOUT-TOWN, *then* CISSIE, *and so on.*]

KHARUDA
Mule! Camel! Dog! Pig! Fawn!

[*Light on their faces shows the change one by one.*

AMUSEMENTS OF KHAN KHARUDA

BESSIE *sits there with a mule's head, the* 2ND MAN-ABOUT-TOWN *has a camel's head,* CISSIE *a dog's head, the* 1ST MAN-ABOUT-TOWN *a pig's head, and* YVONNE *the head of a fawn.*

The portrayal of their feelings on such an occasion is best left to the actors. The lights in the room come back slowly, one by one.

The WAITER *has taken a bottle from its concealment among his clothes and pushed it away, overtaken by sudden honesty and a still greater distrust of wine.*]

KHARUDA [*still standing, with his demon's face*]
It is enough.

[*He raises his arm slowly upwards as he had moved it slowly downwards. Thunder follows it and darkness as before. And then the thunder ripples away fainter and fainter as though going back to remote hills.*

Light, and the faces all human again.]

KHARUDA
Waiter. A jolly old drink, please.

[*The* WAITER *brings the bottle he had abstracted and pours with a trembling hand in the silence.*]

BESSIE
I, I think I'll have one too.

[*The* WAITER *helps her and passes on to the others.*]

AMUSEMENTS OF KHAN KHARUDA

2ND MAN-ABOUT-TOWN

I say, Charlie; really after this bottle we oughtn't to have any more champagne. Eh?

1ST MAN-ABOUT-TOWN

Well, no. Not after this one.
[*Both drink.*]

Curtain

www.ingramcontent.com/pod-product-compliance
Lightning Source LLC
LaVergne TN
LVHW041617070426
835507LV00008B/299